Just for

DESIGN A DRESS

75 Creative Styles

Fashion Dreams
Drawing
& Coloring Book

NOTIKA PASHENKO & SARAH JANISSE BROWN

The Thinking Tree Publishing Company LLC 2016
Copyright 2016 Do Not Copy
FUNSCHOOLINGBOOKS.COM

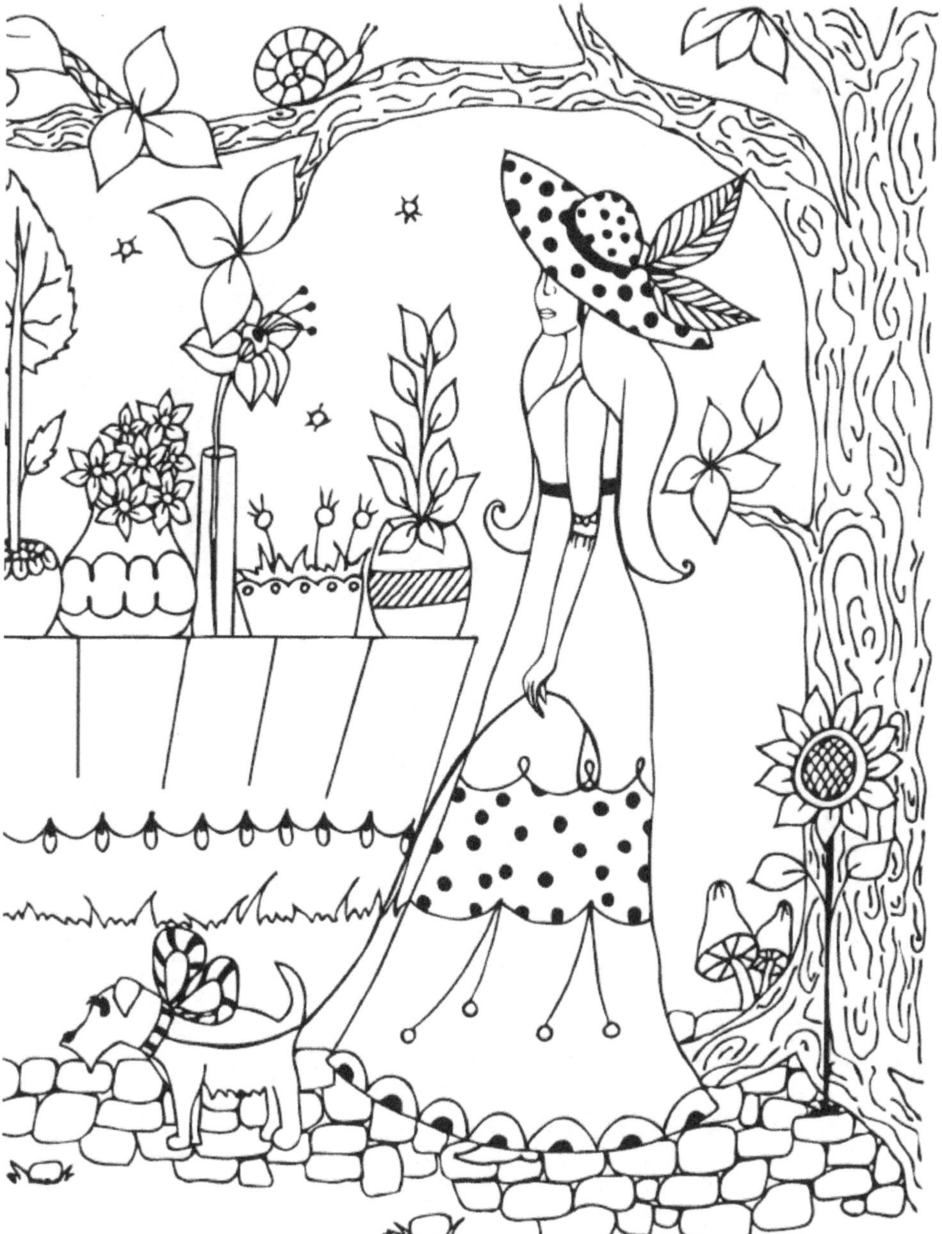

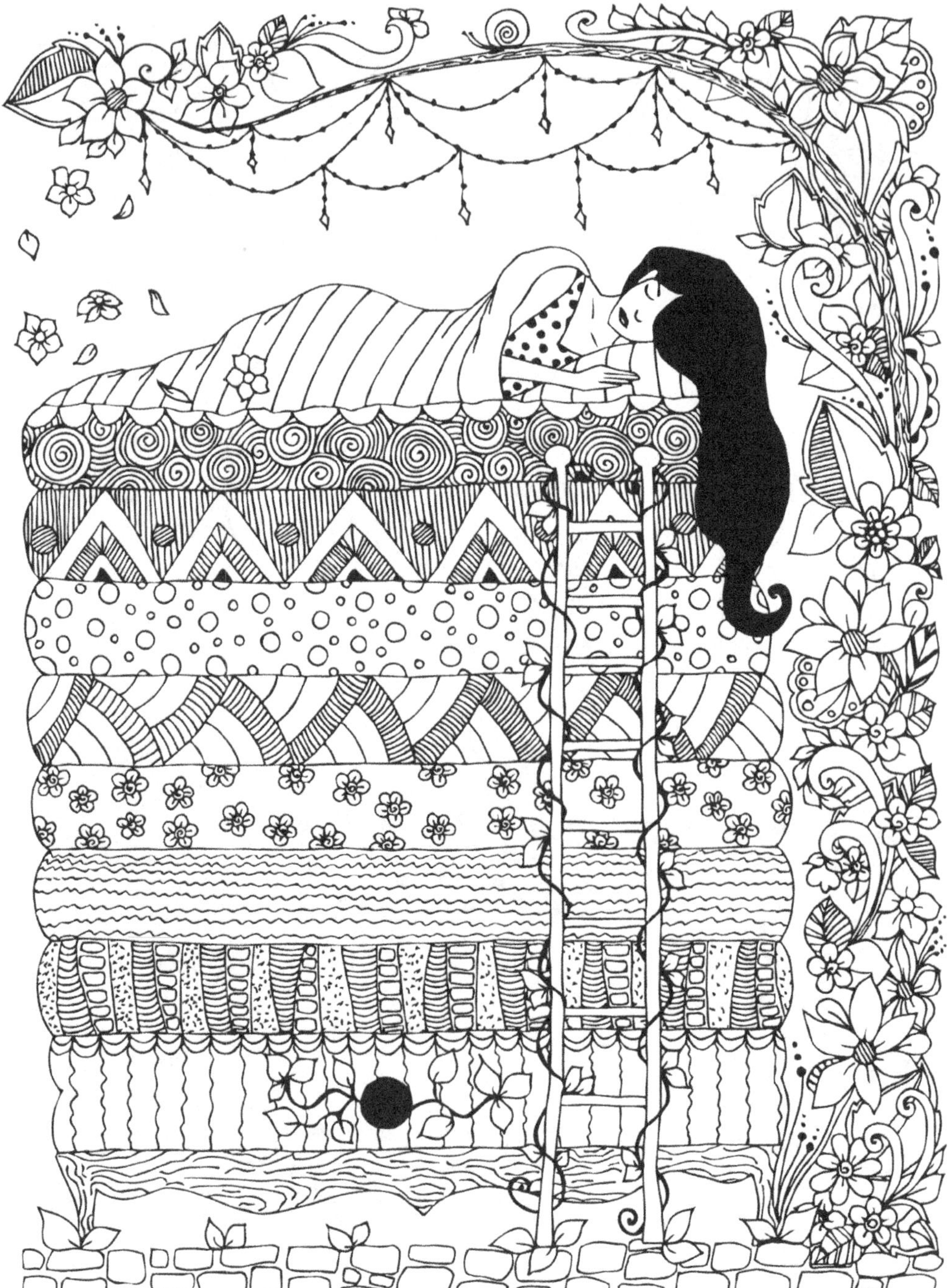

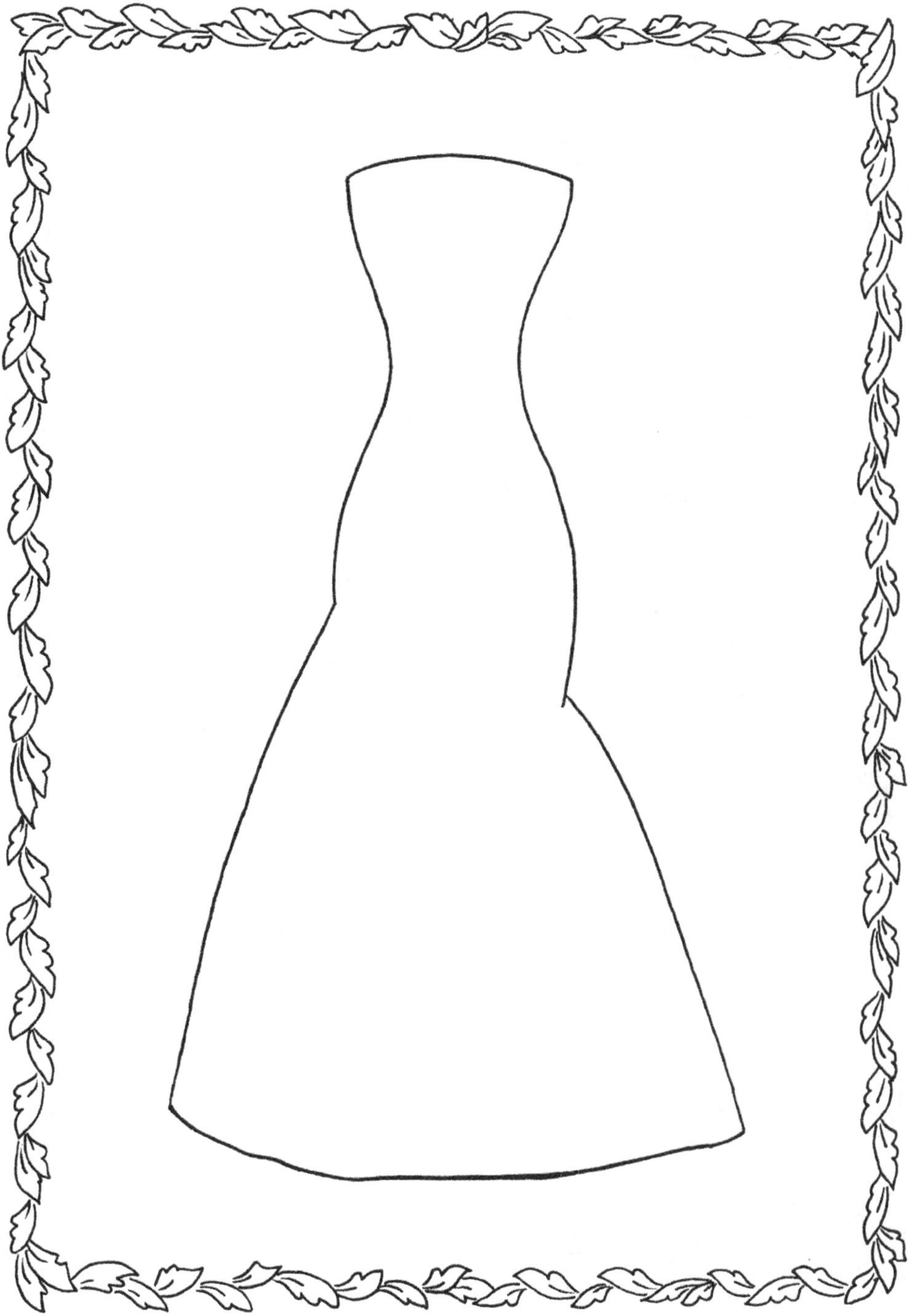

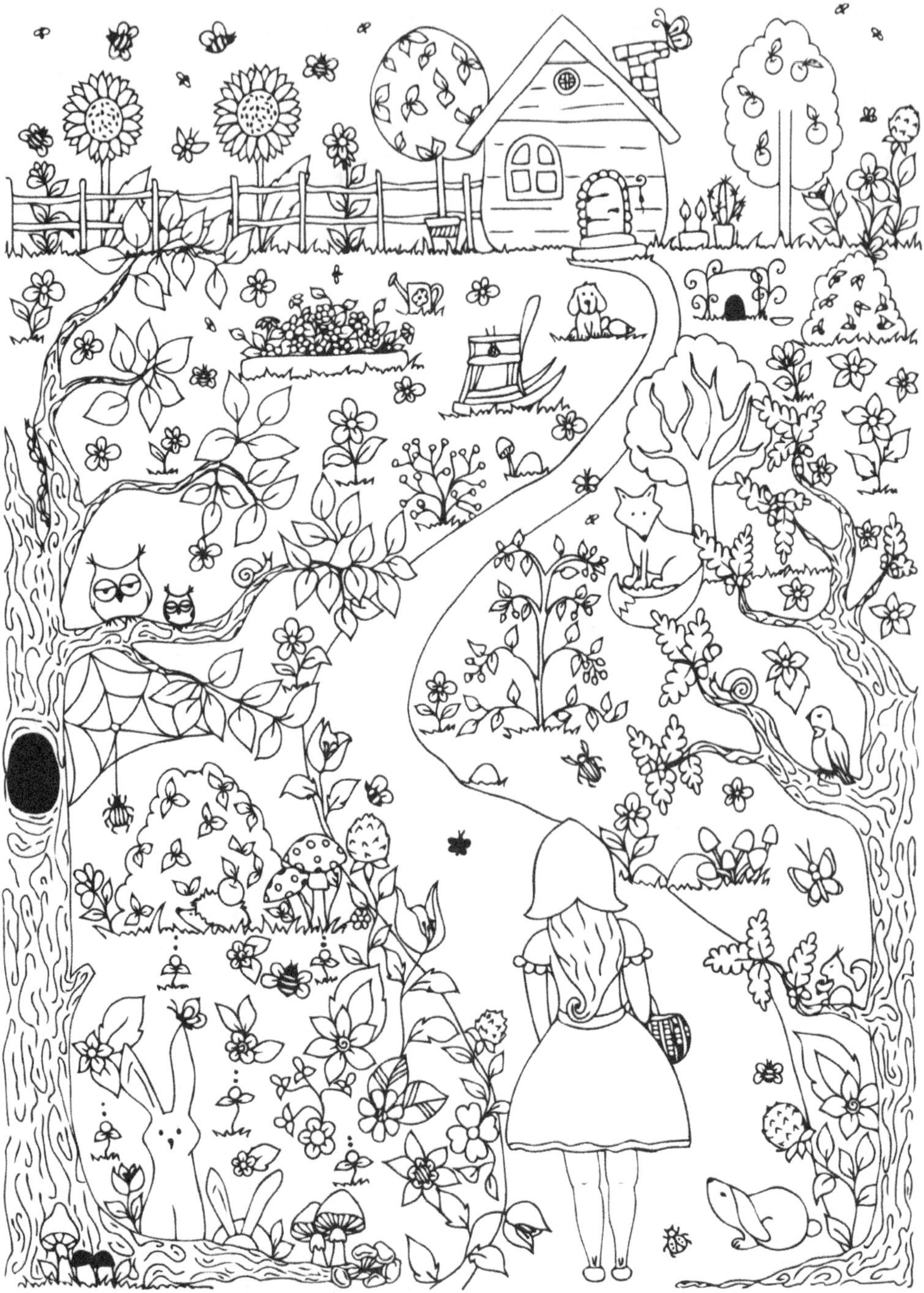

Decorate & Color this Dress

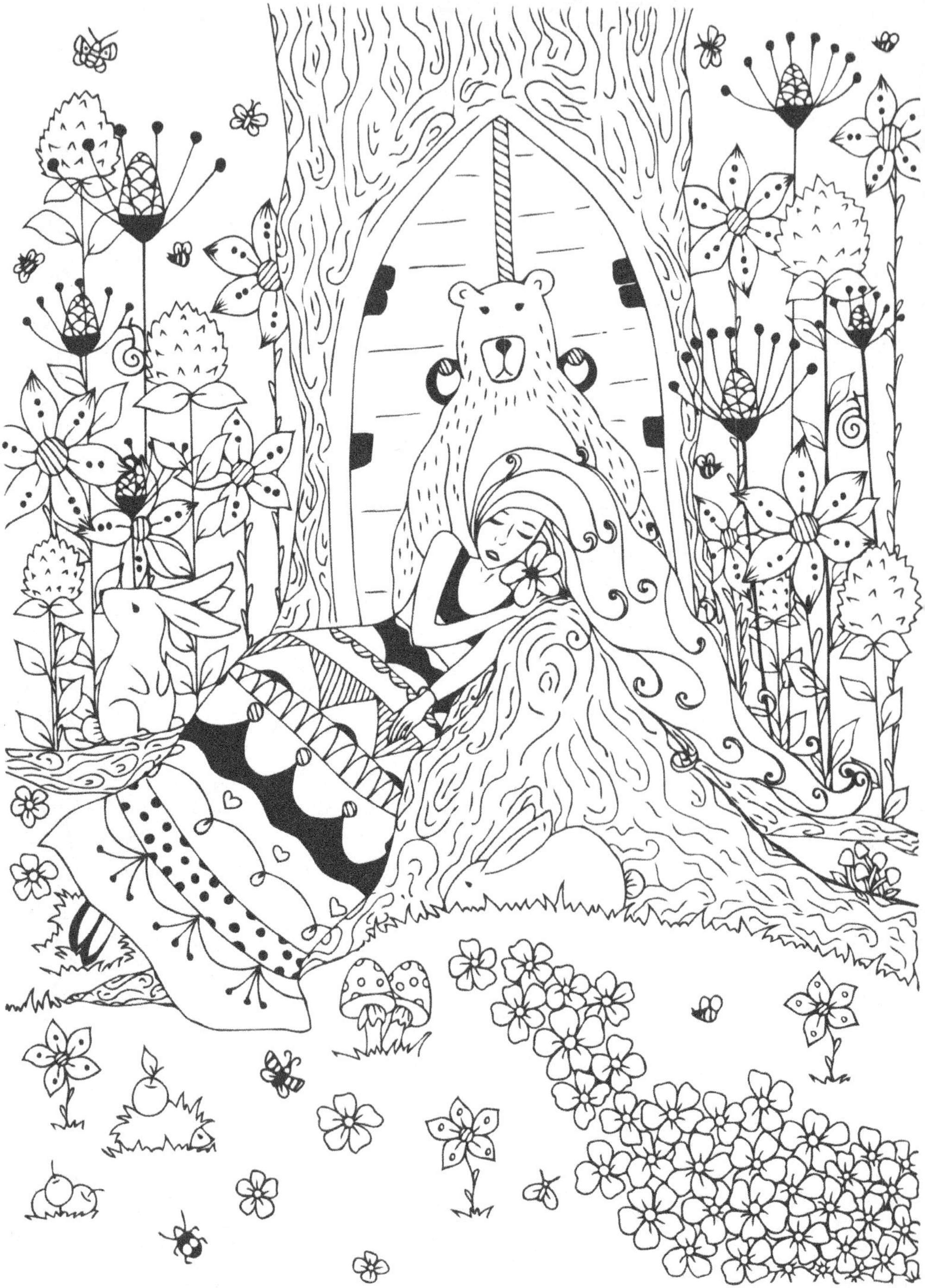

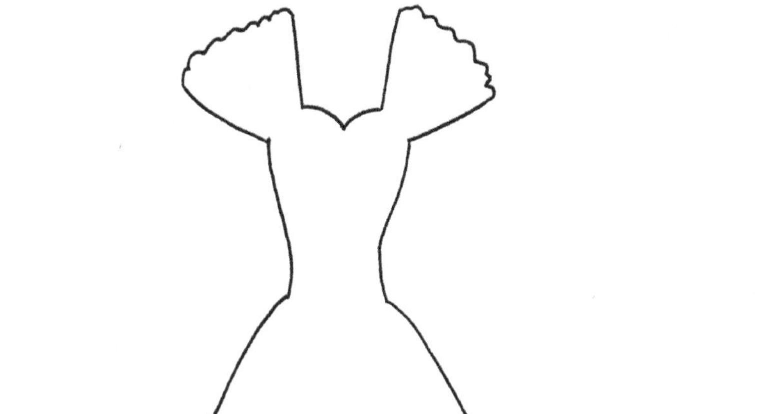

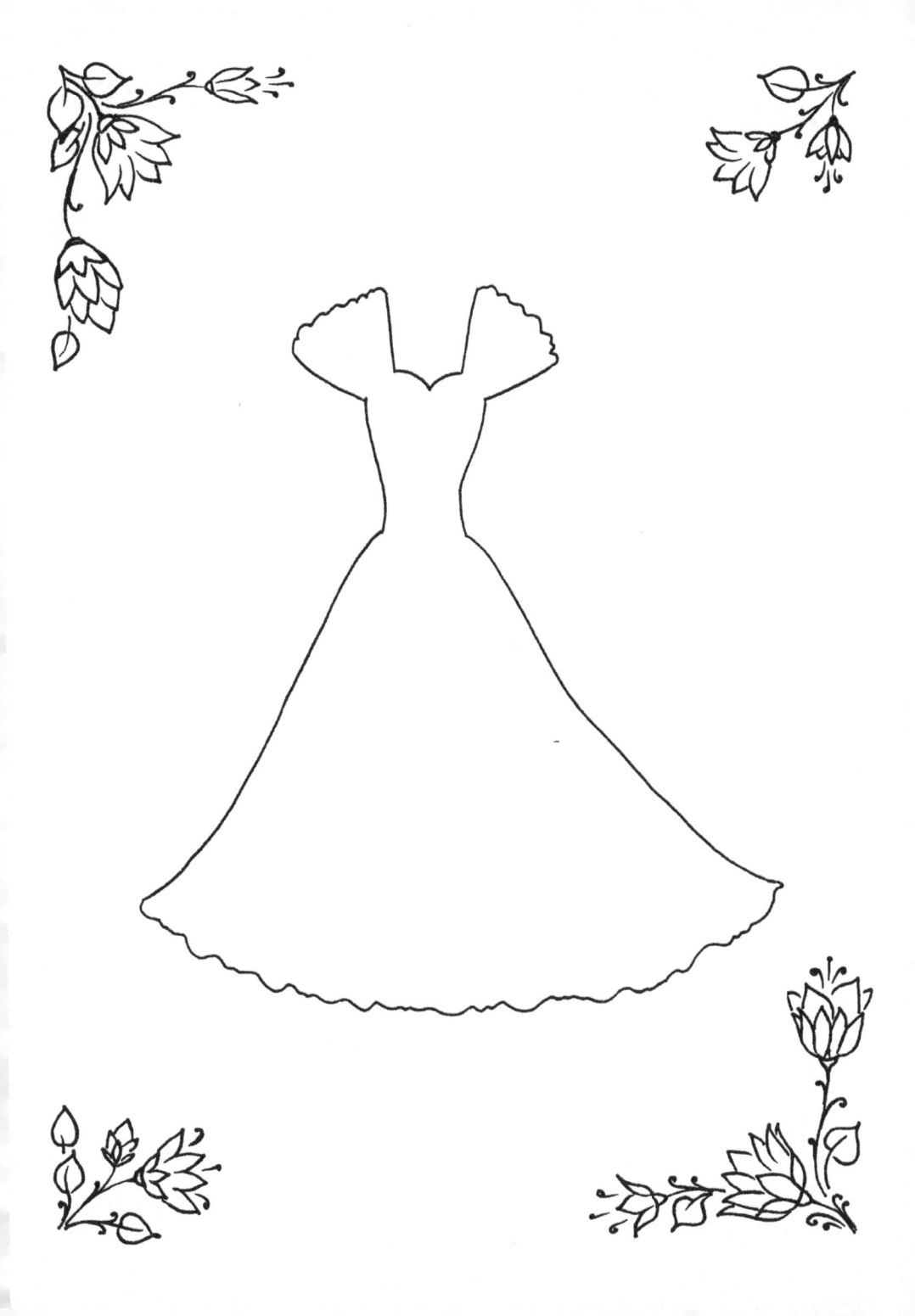

Draw your own Dress

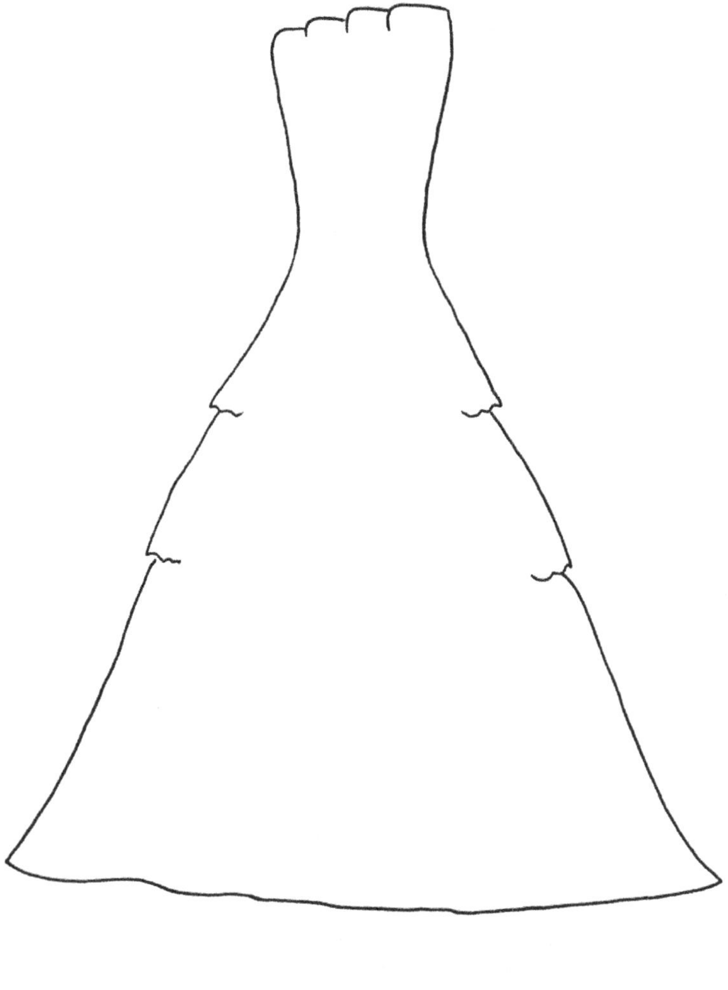

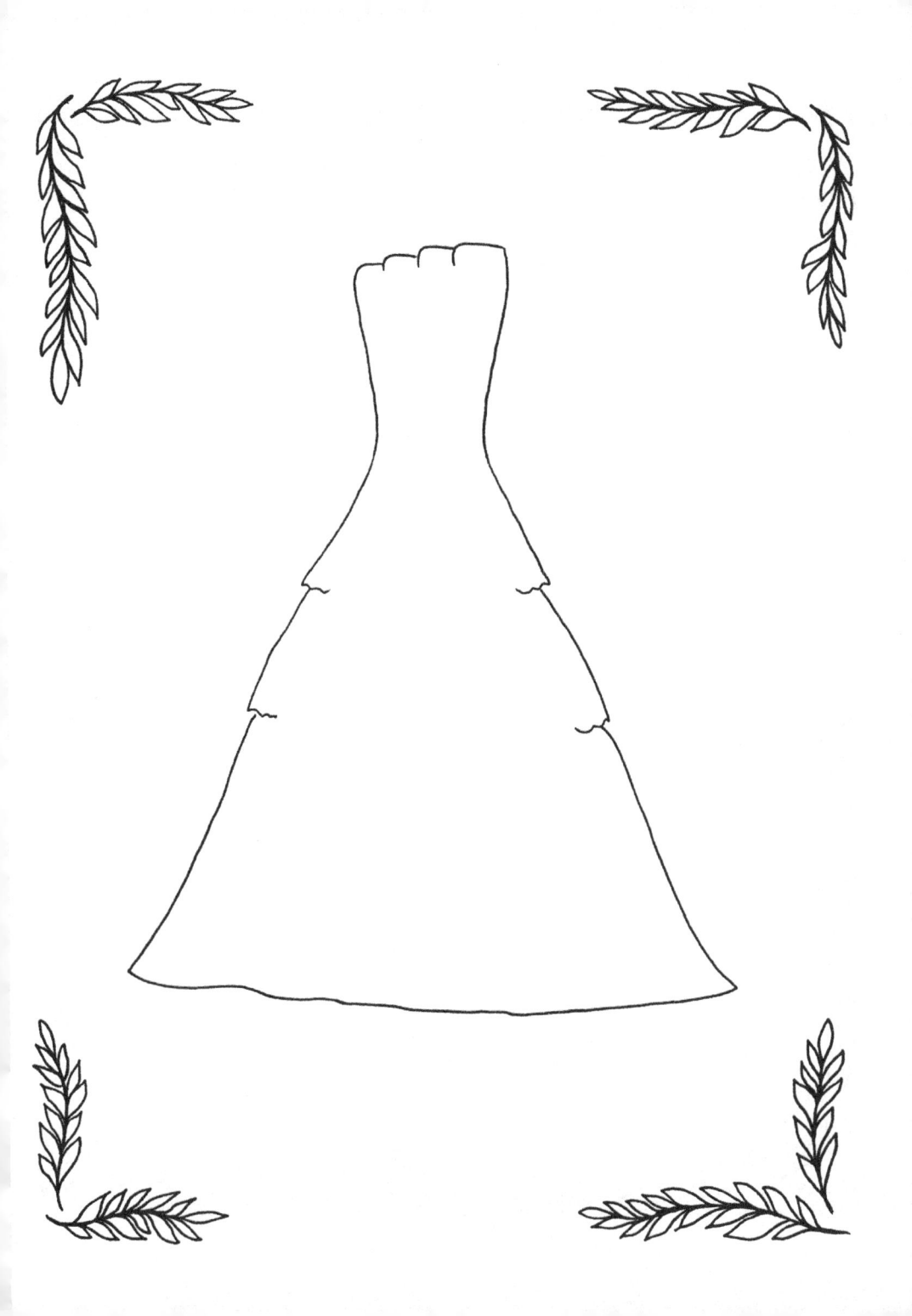

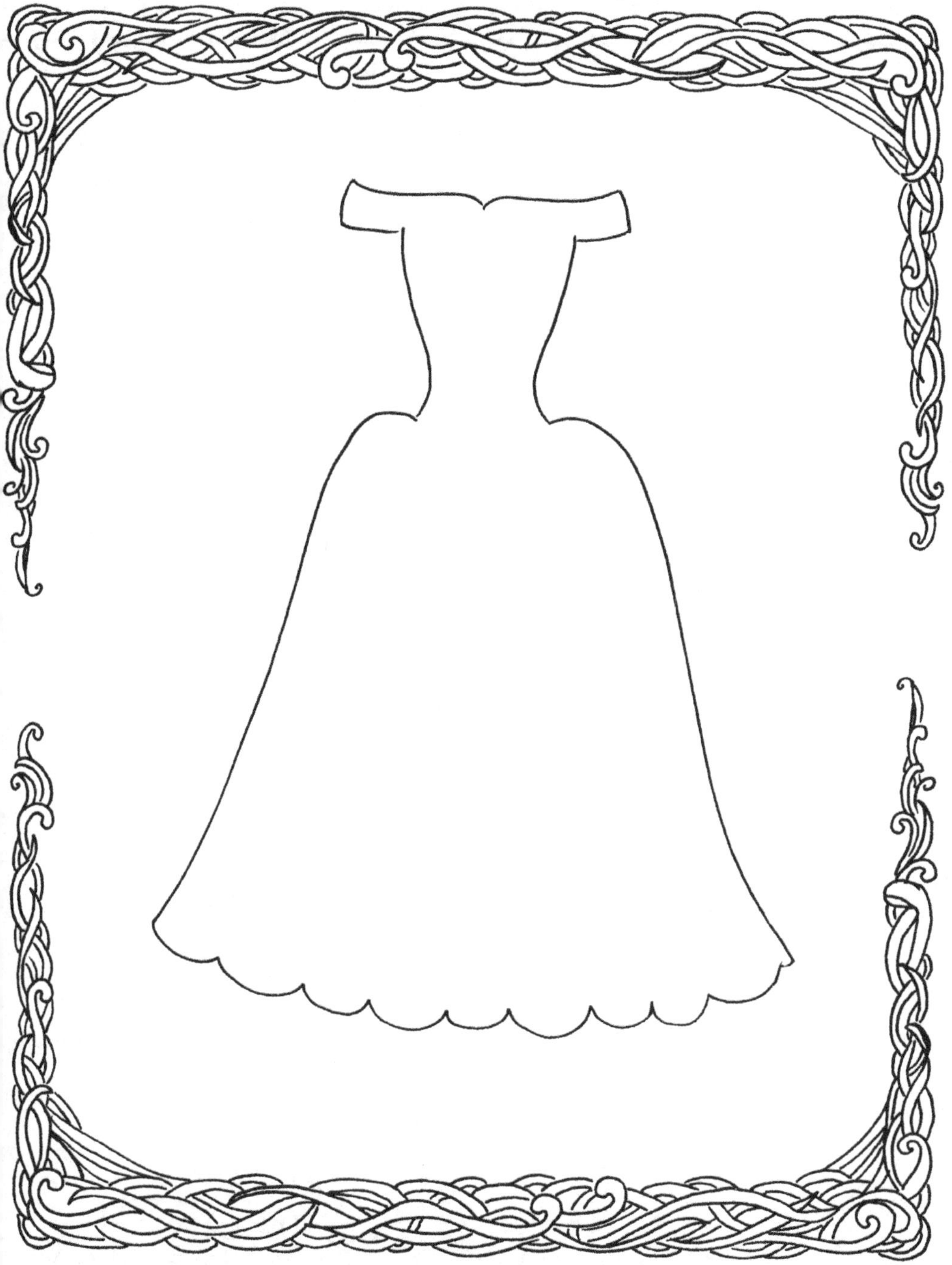

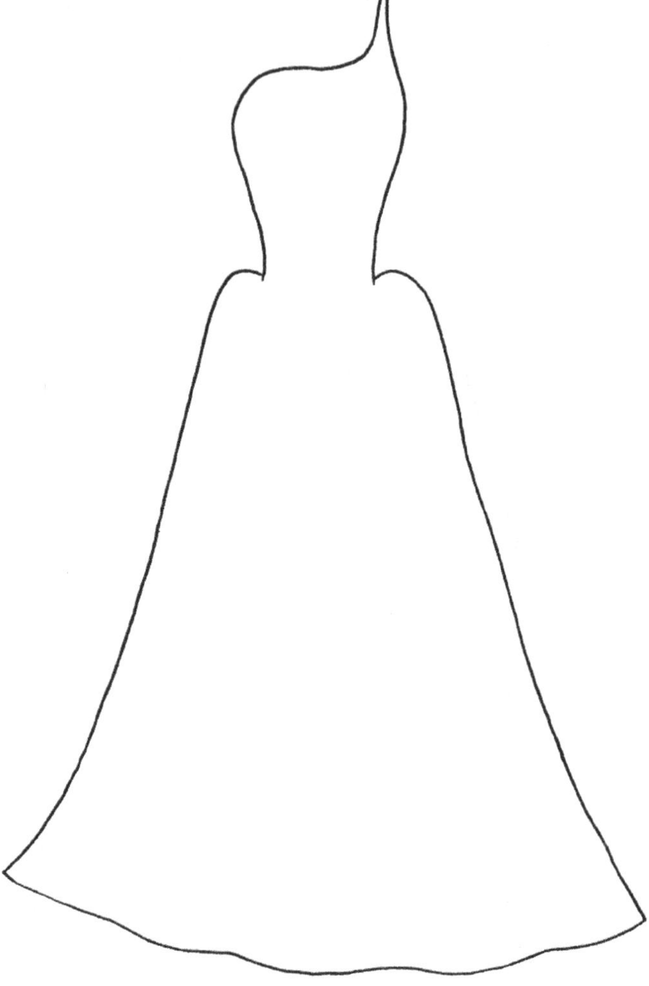

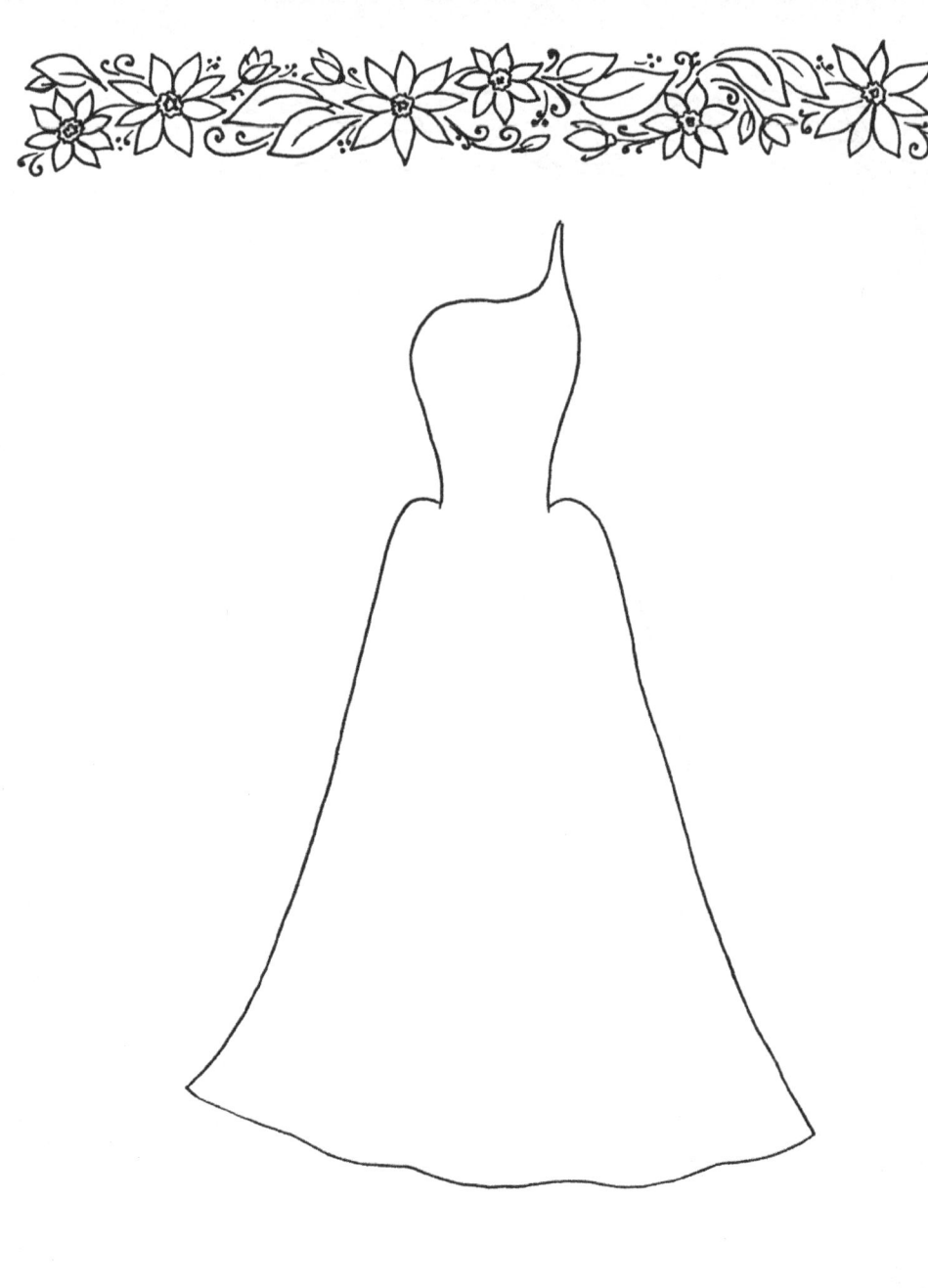

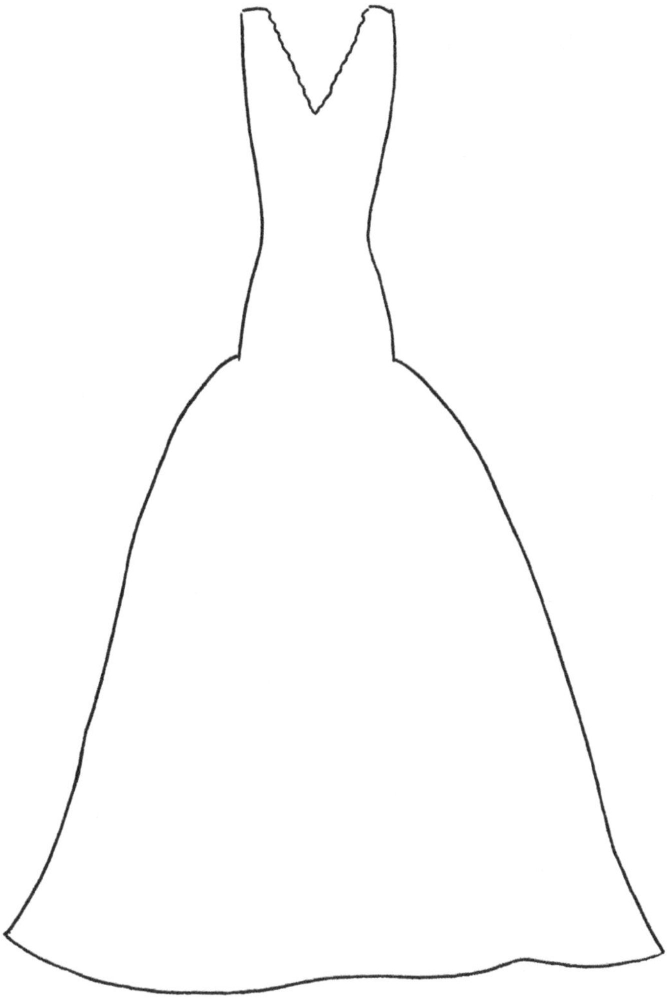

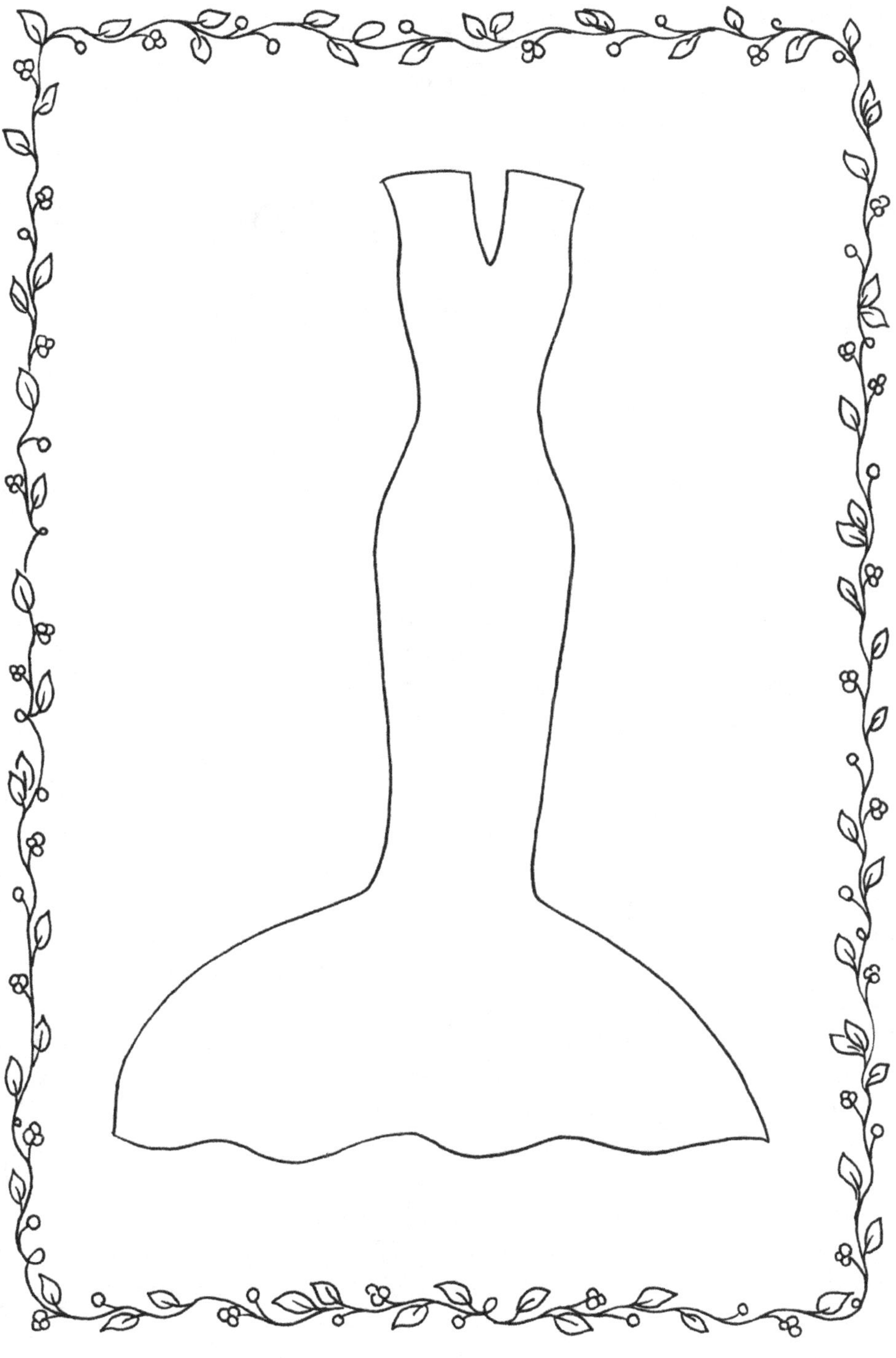

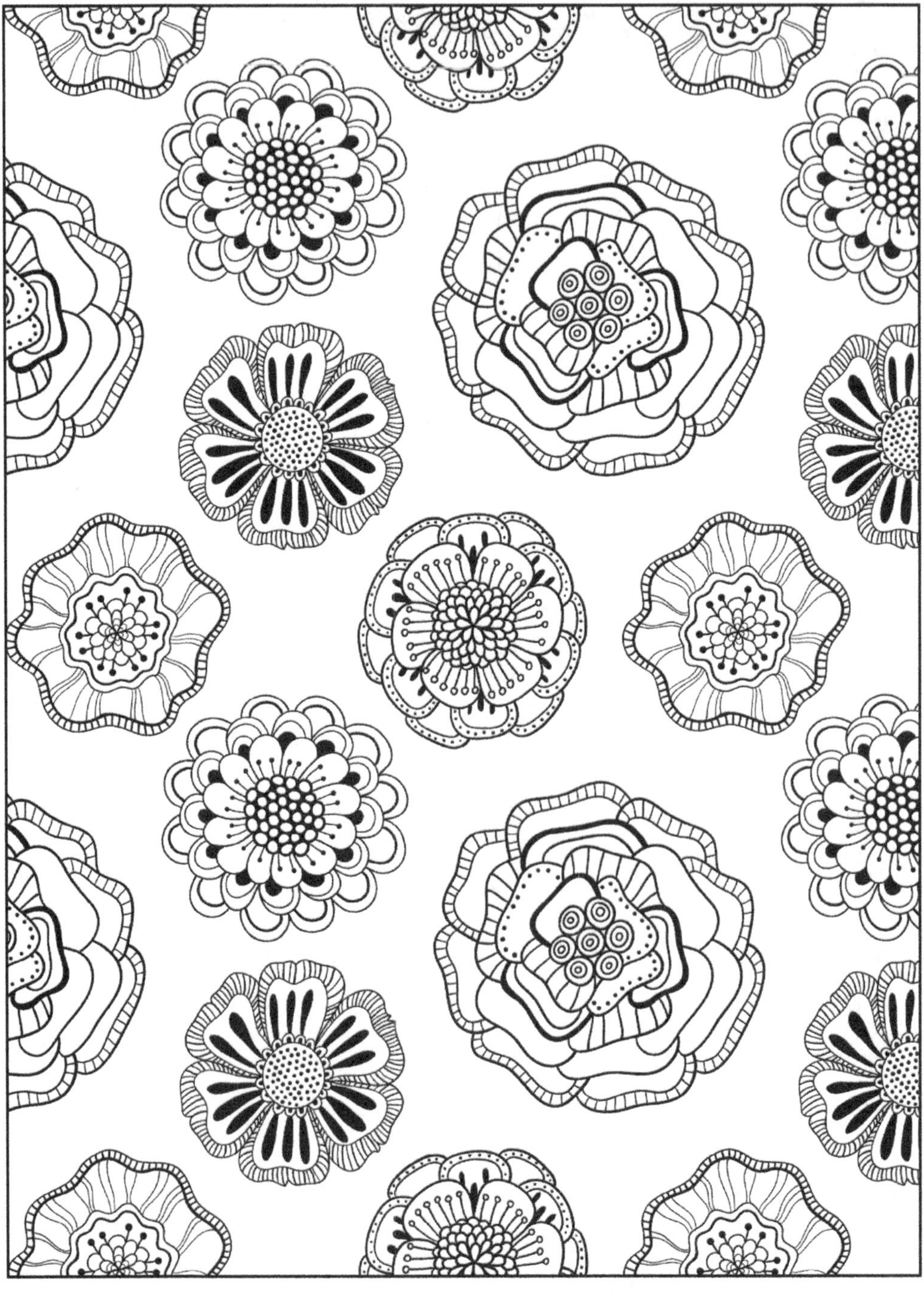

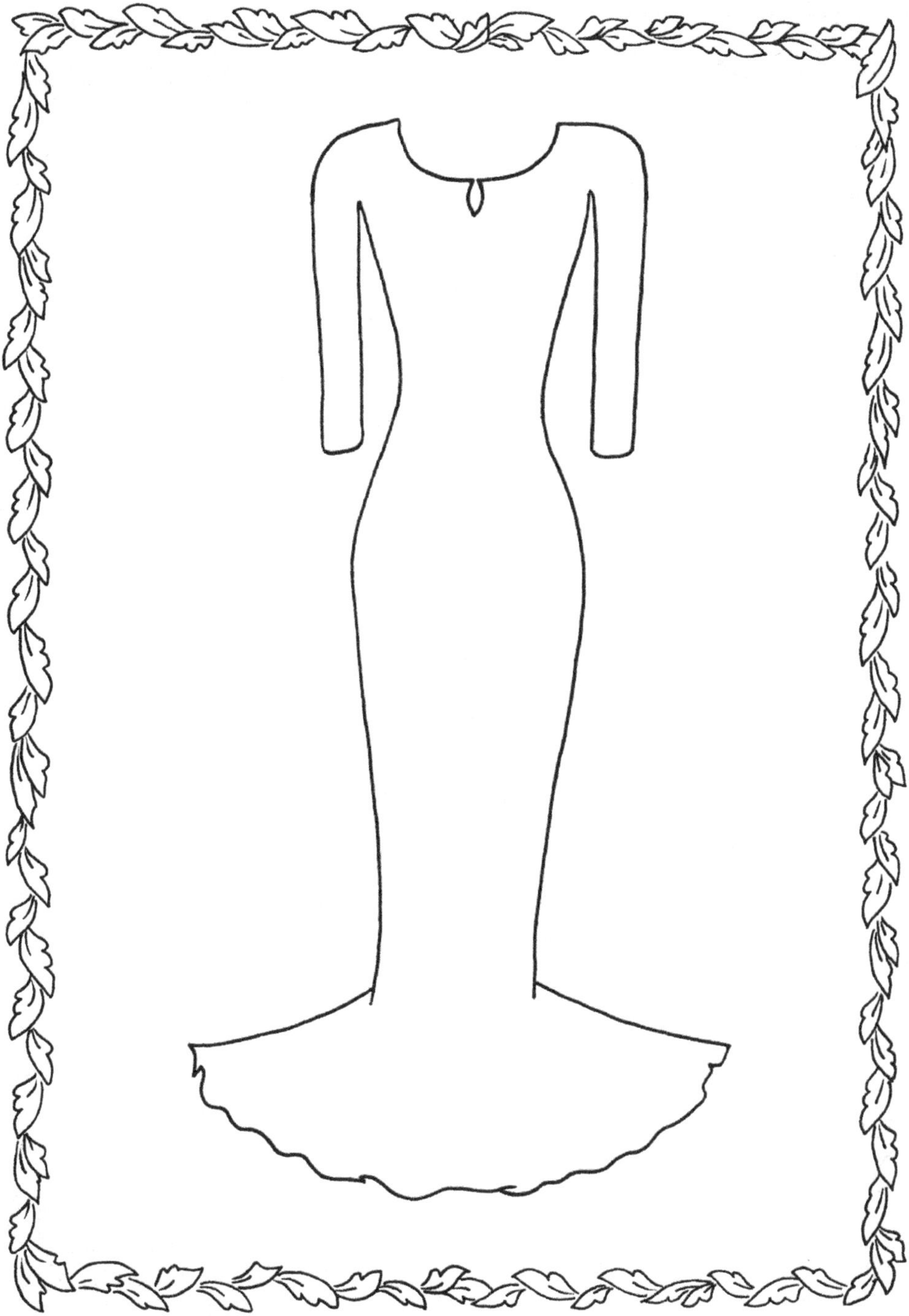

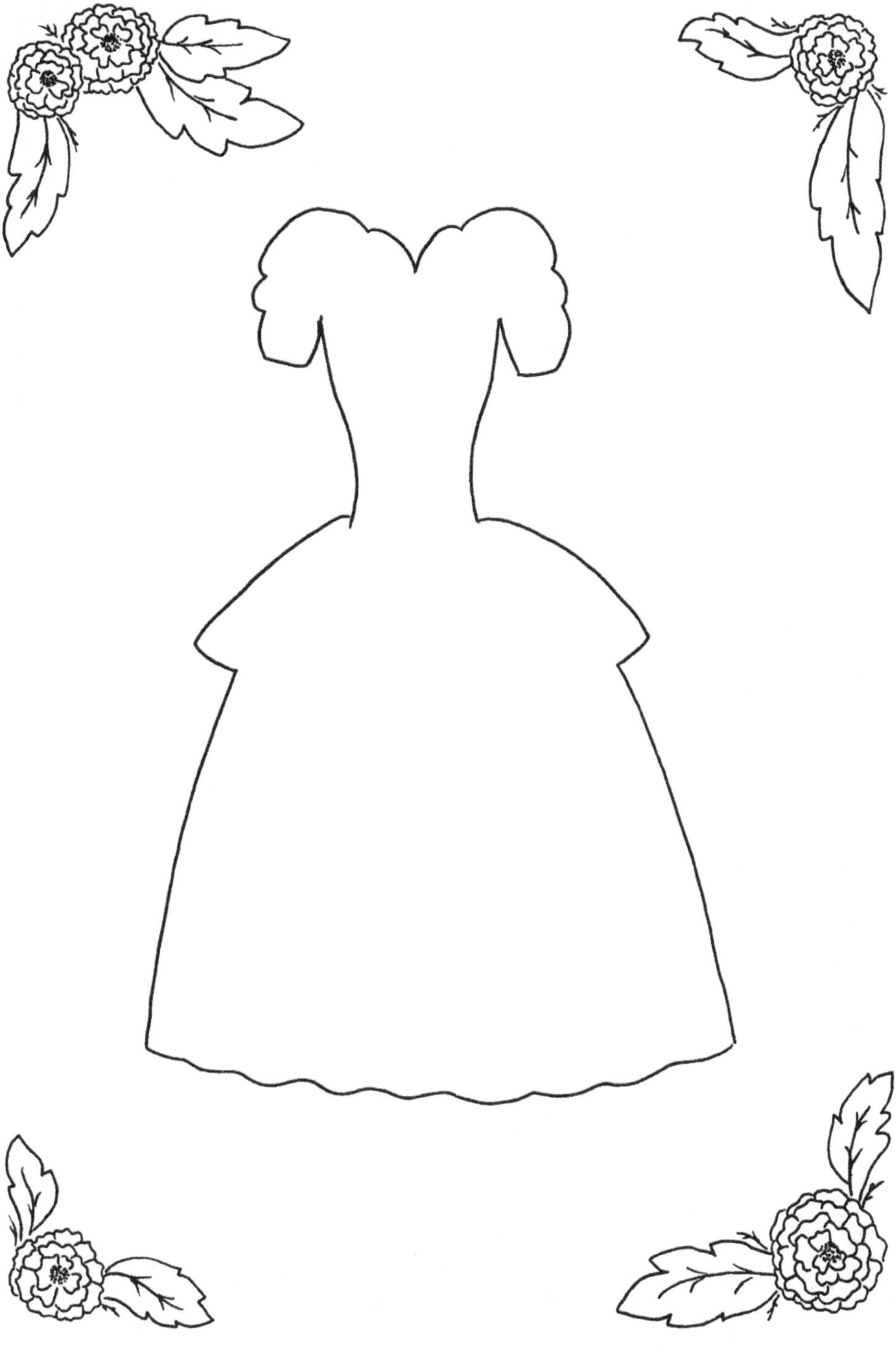

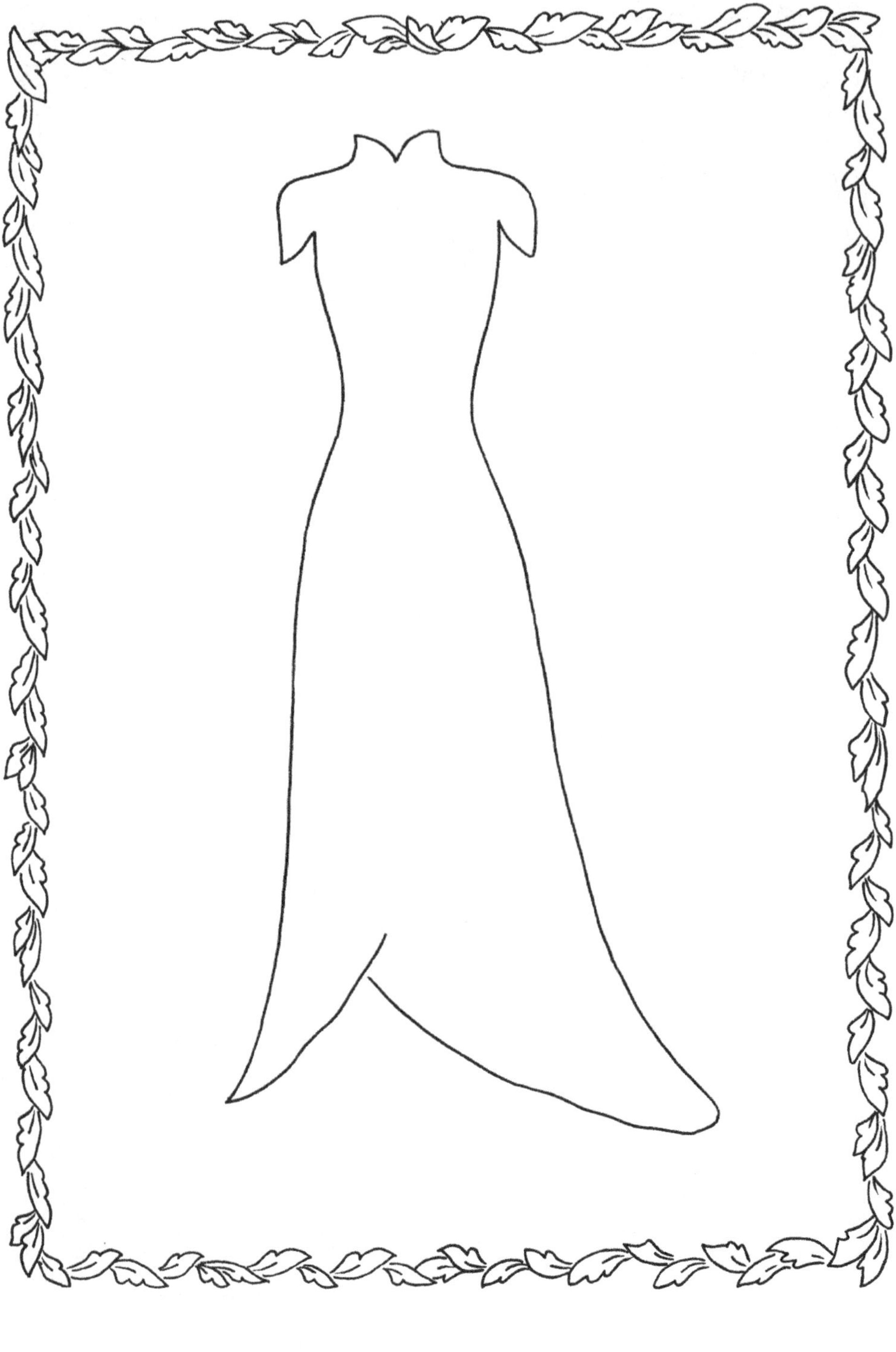

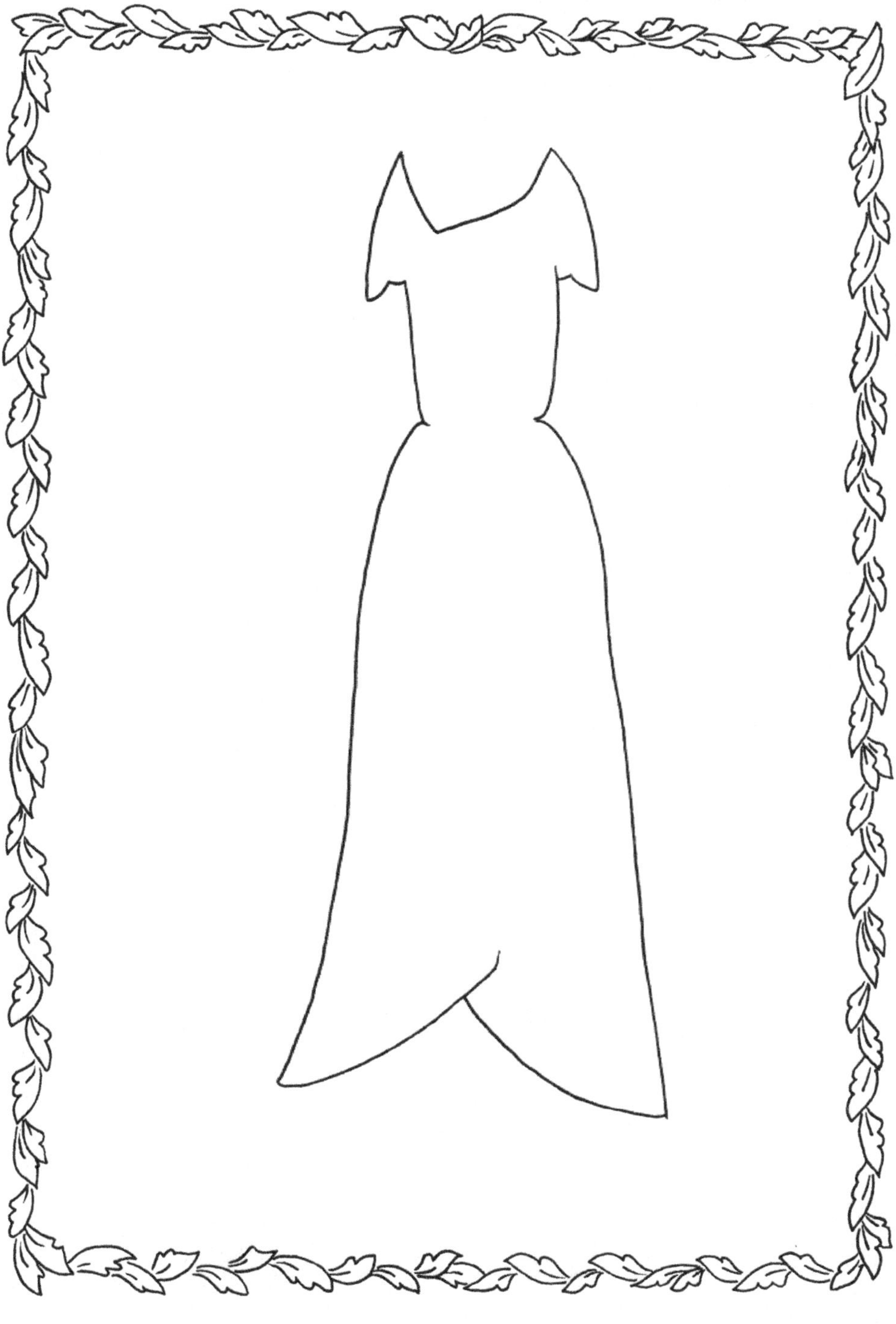

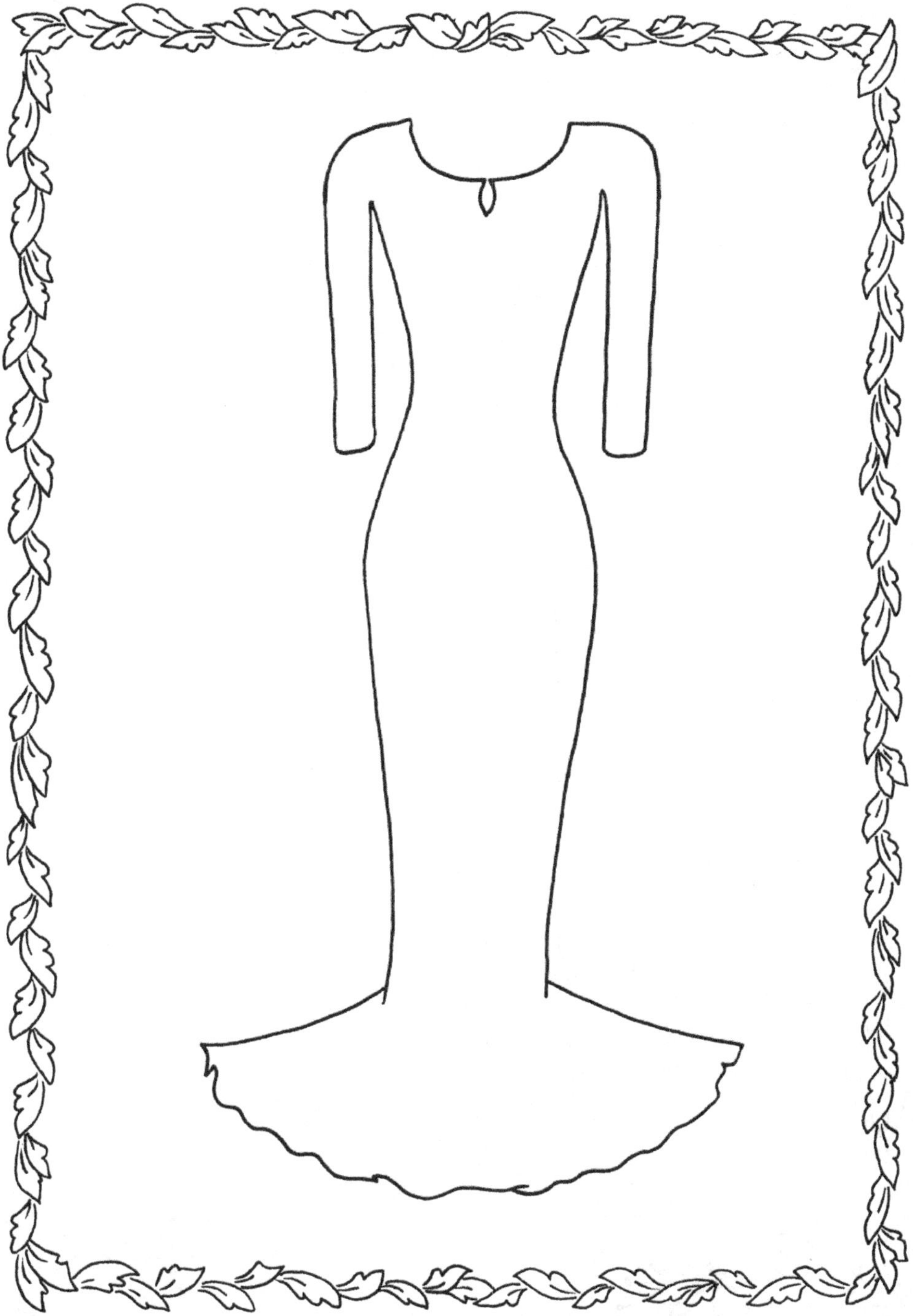

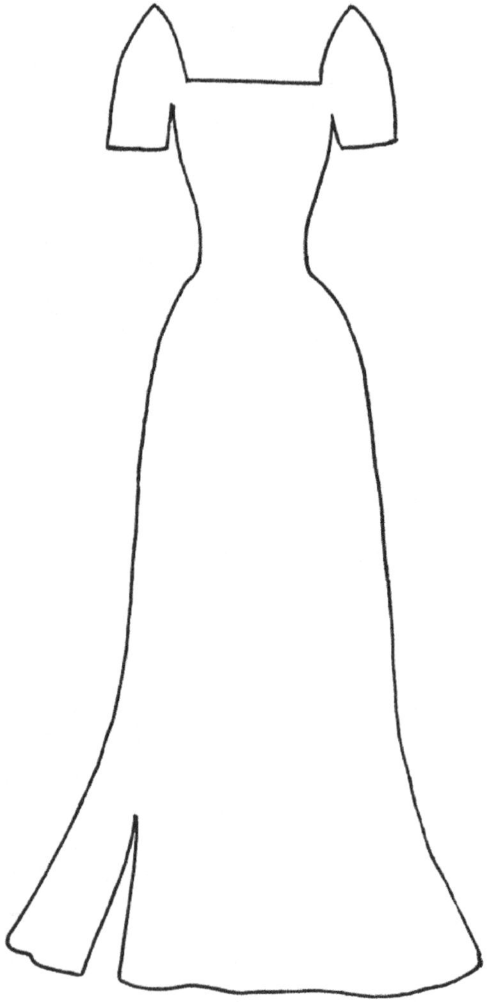

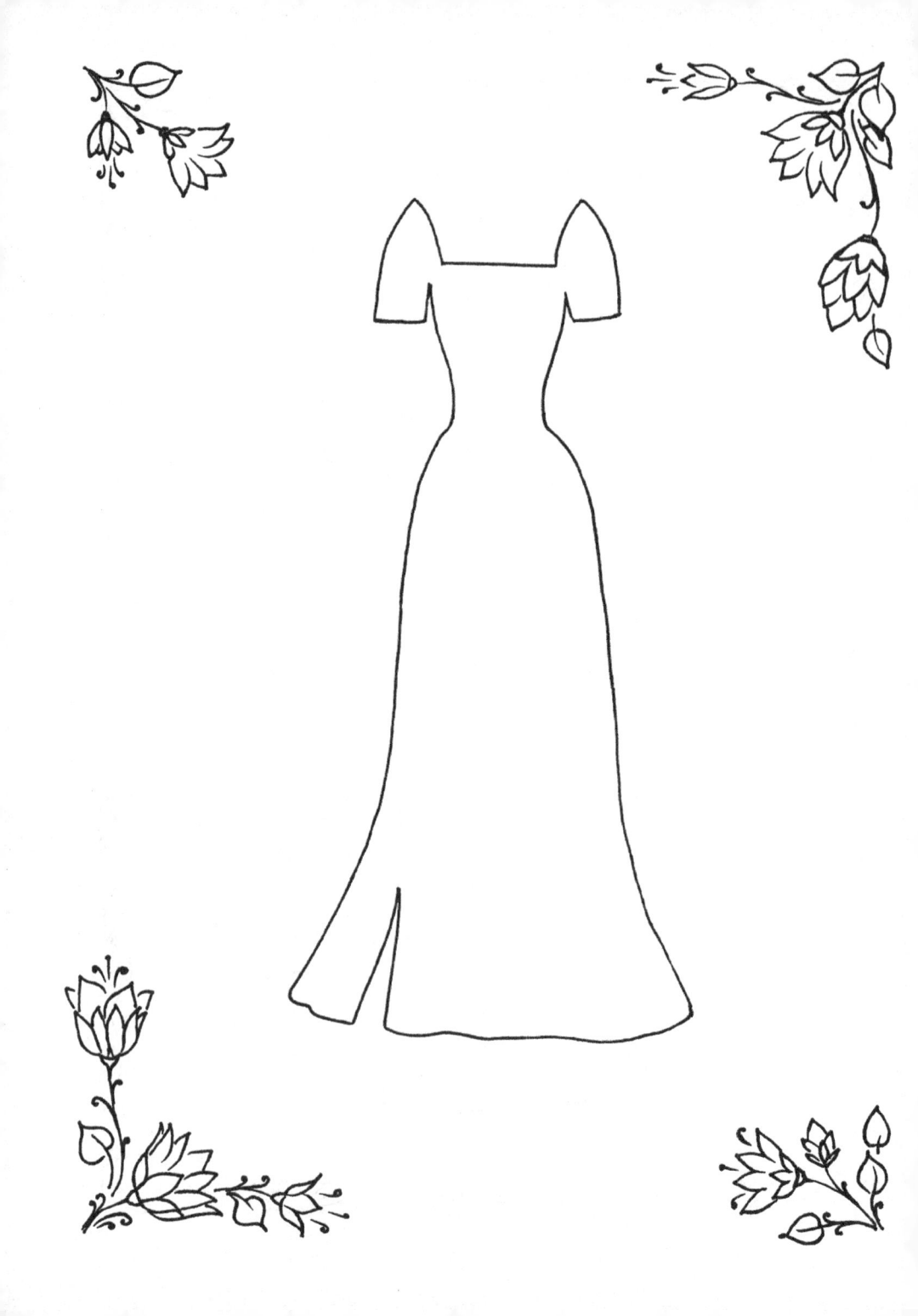

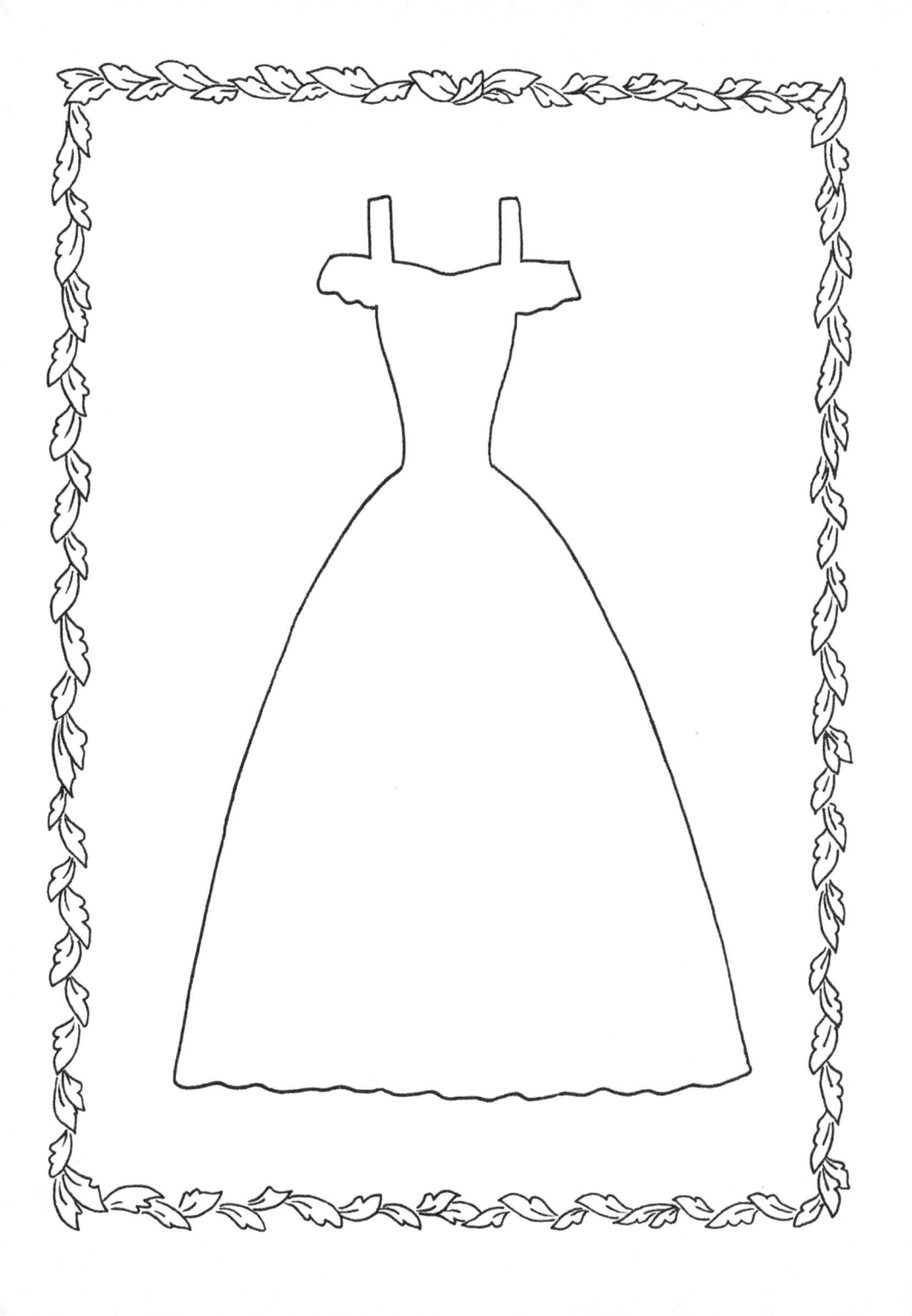

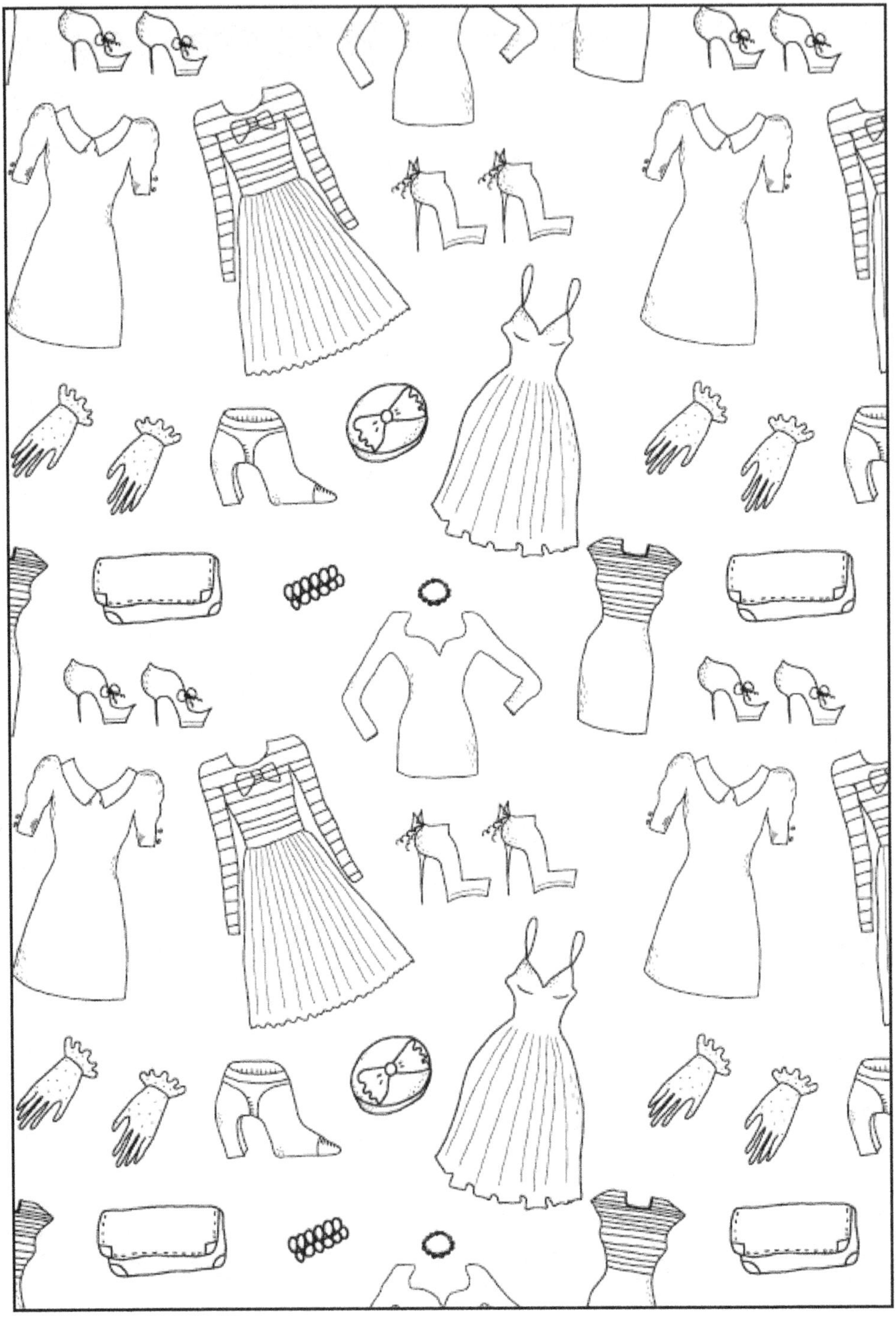

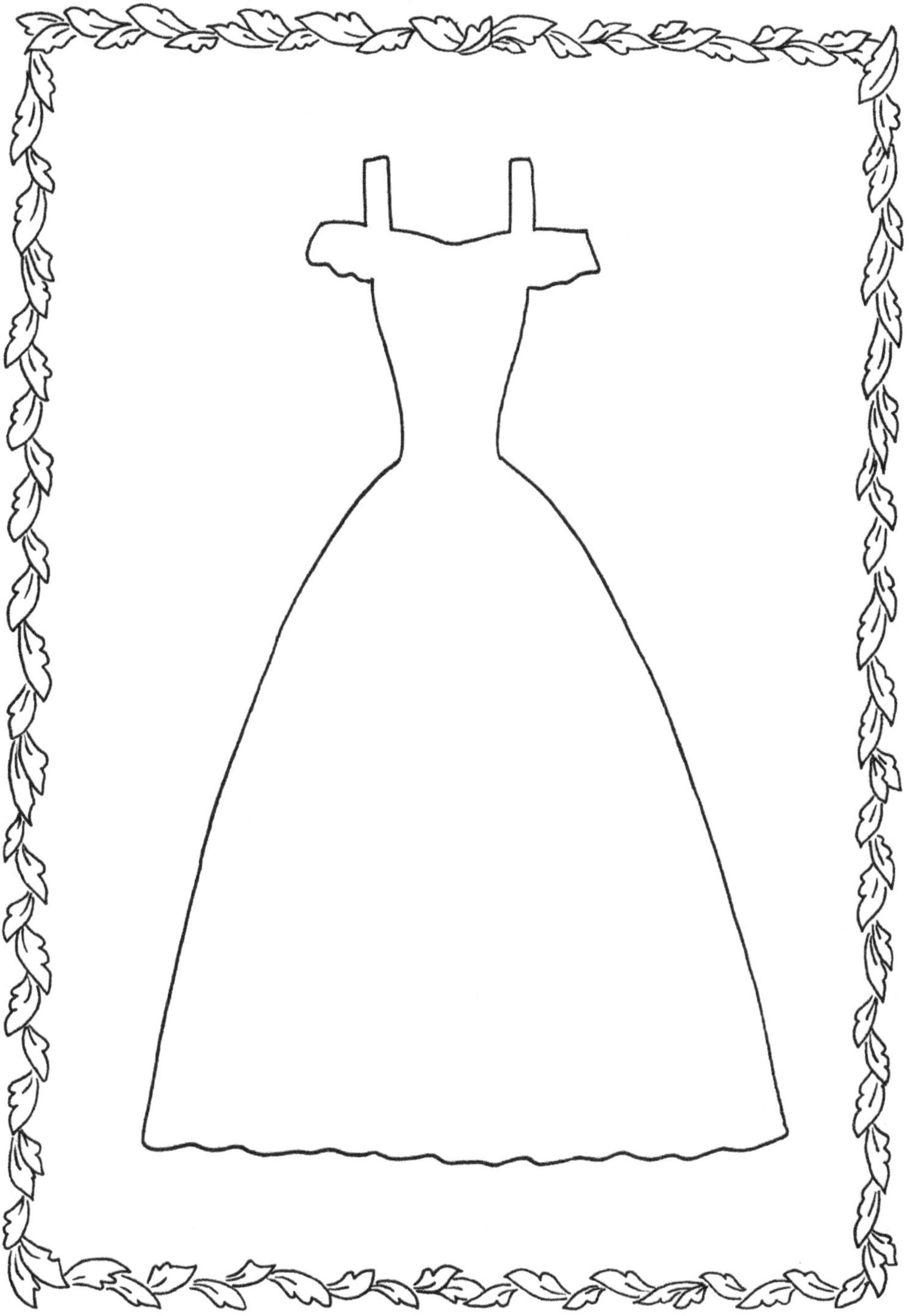

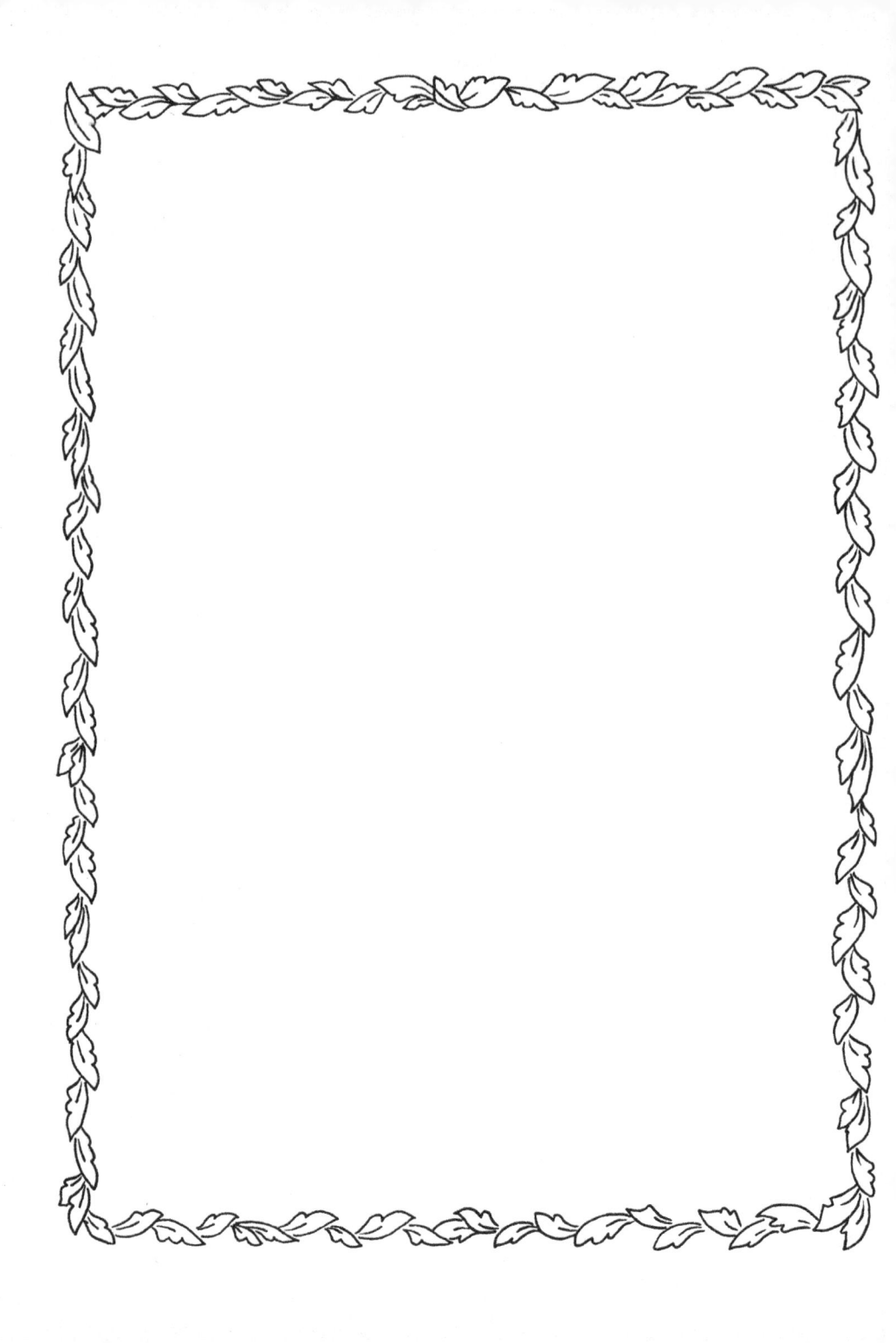

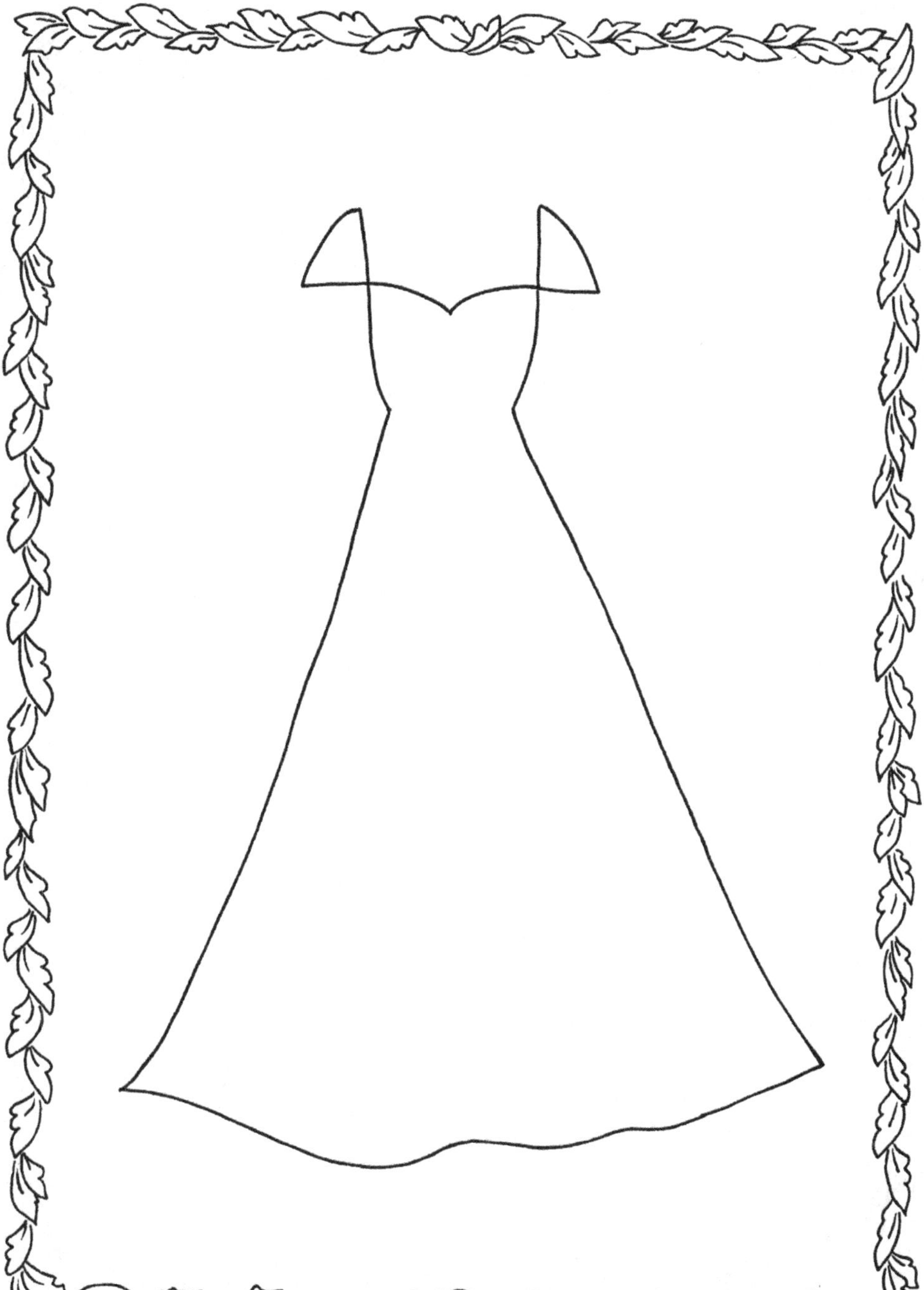

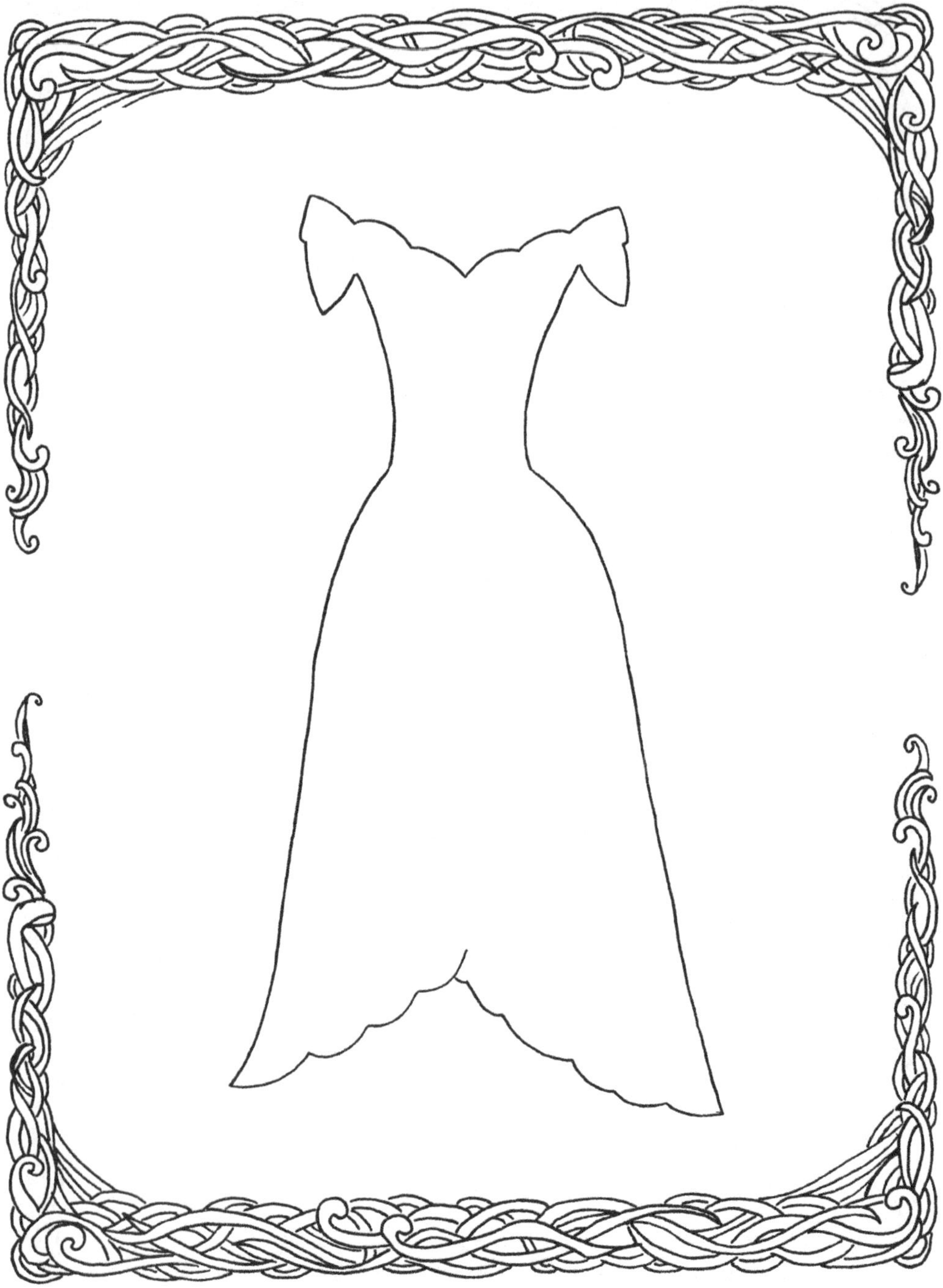

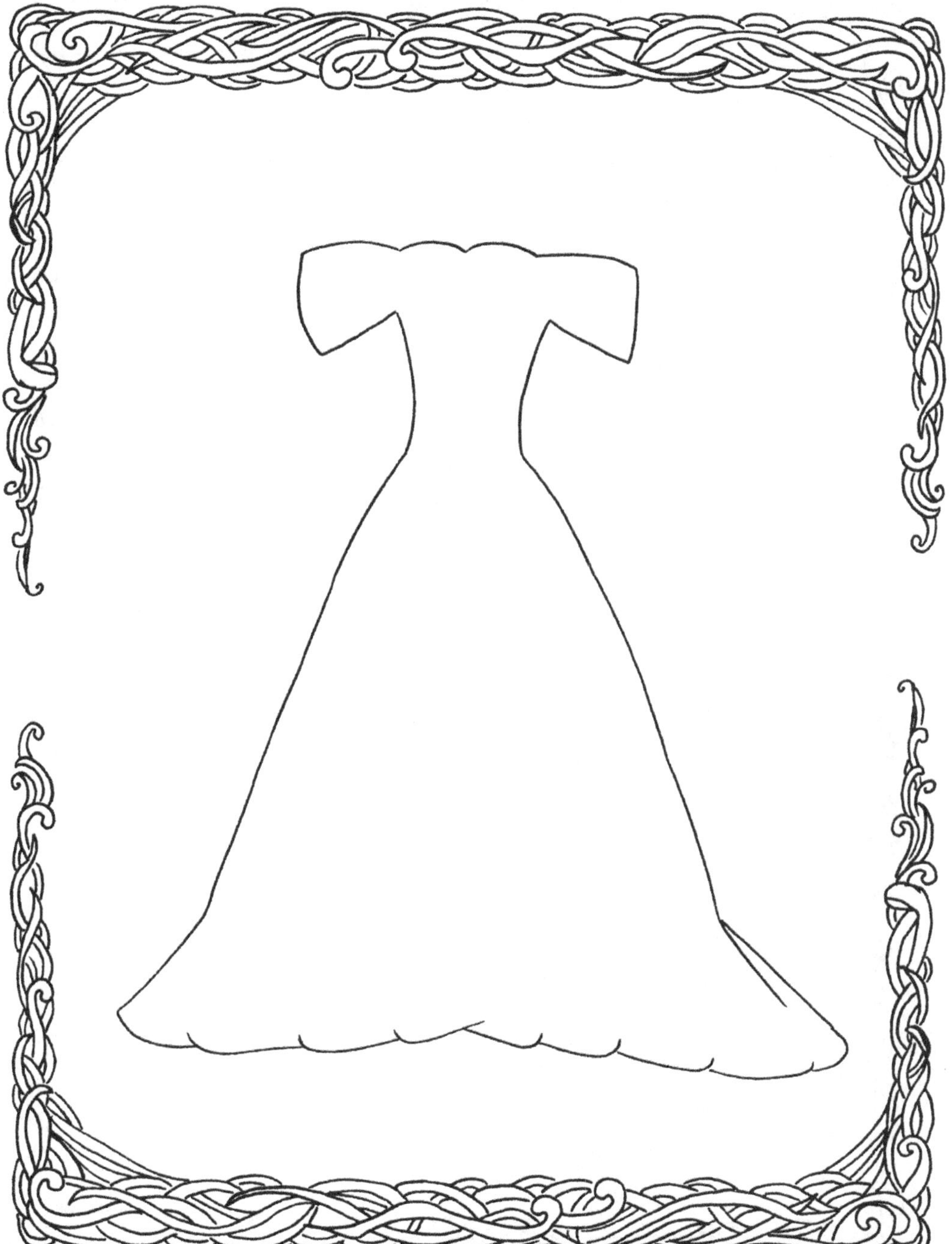

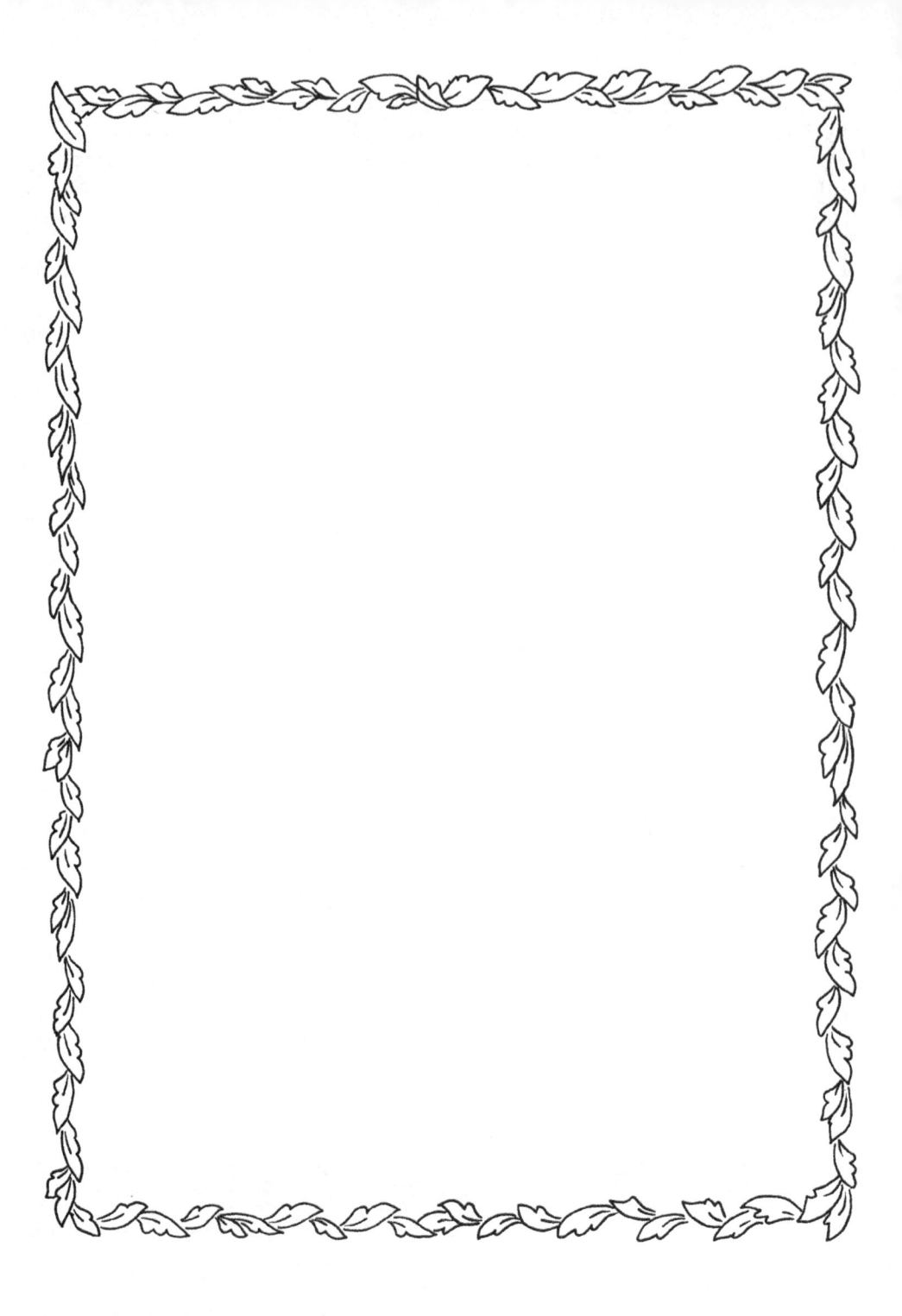

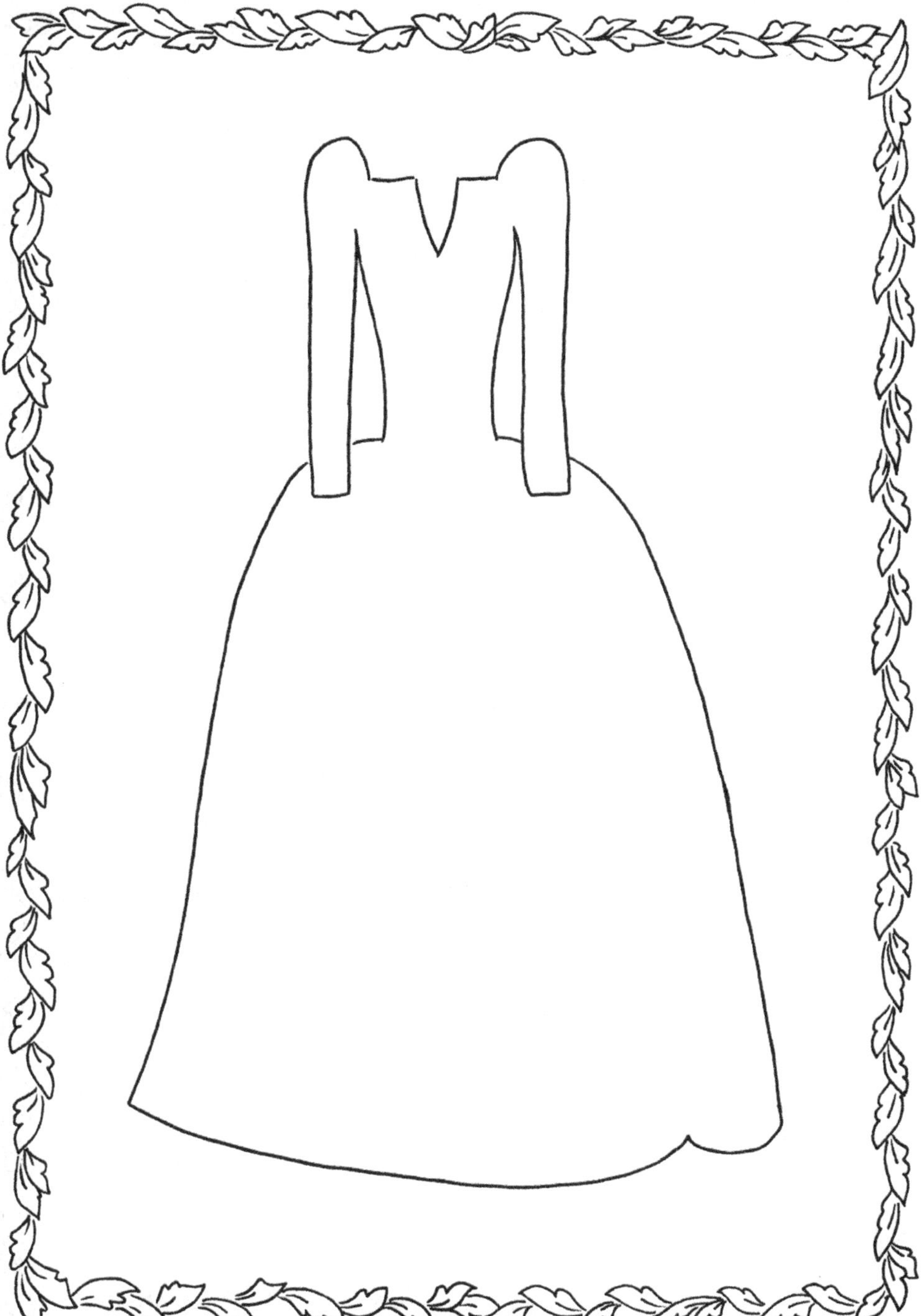

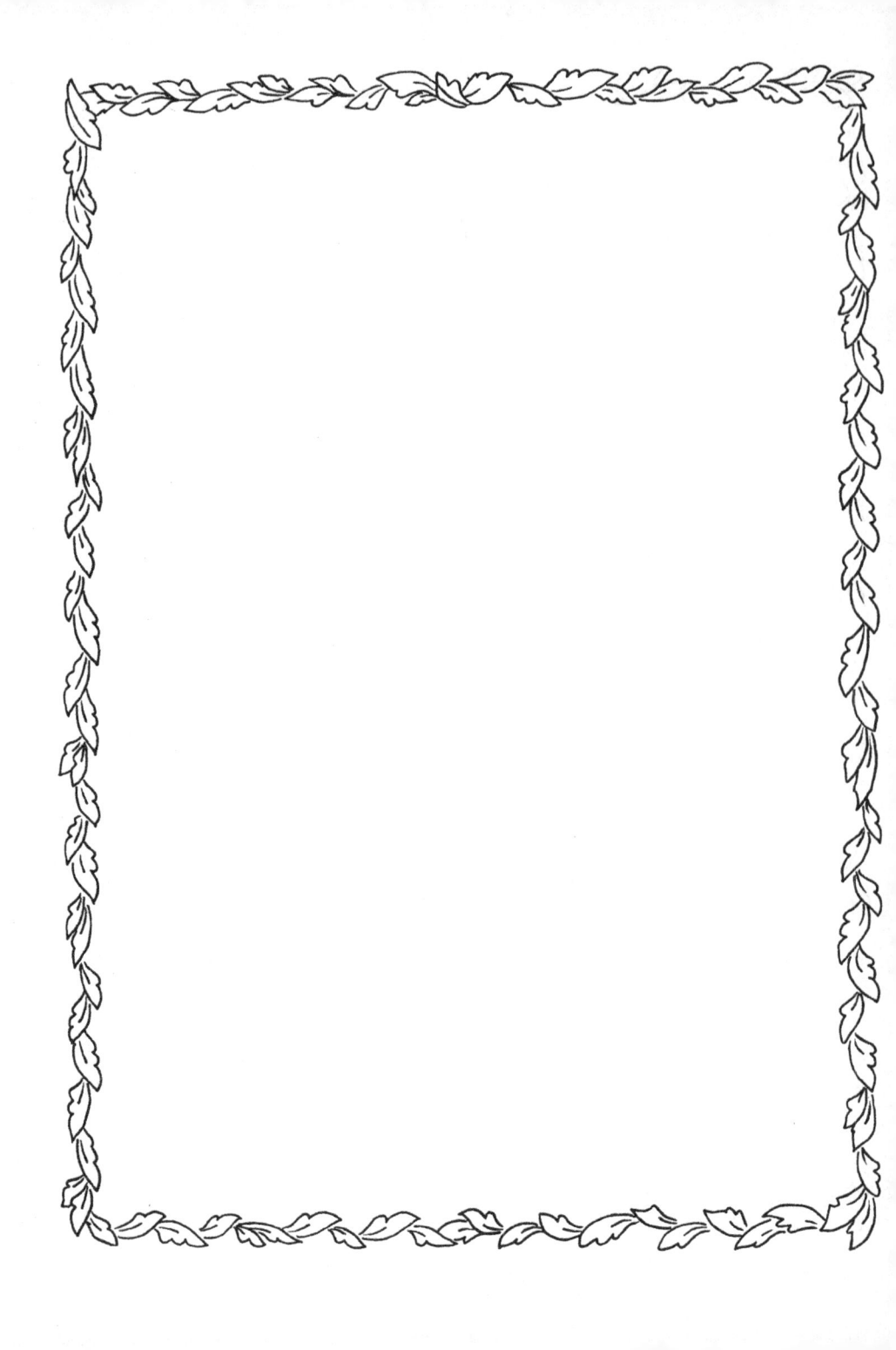

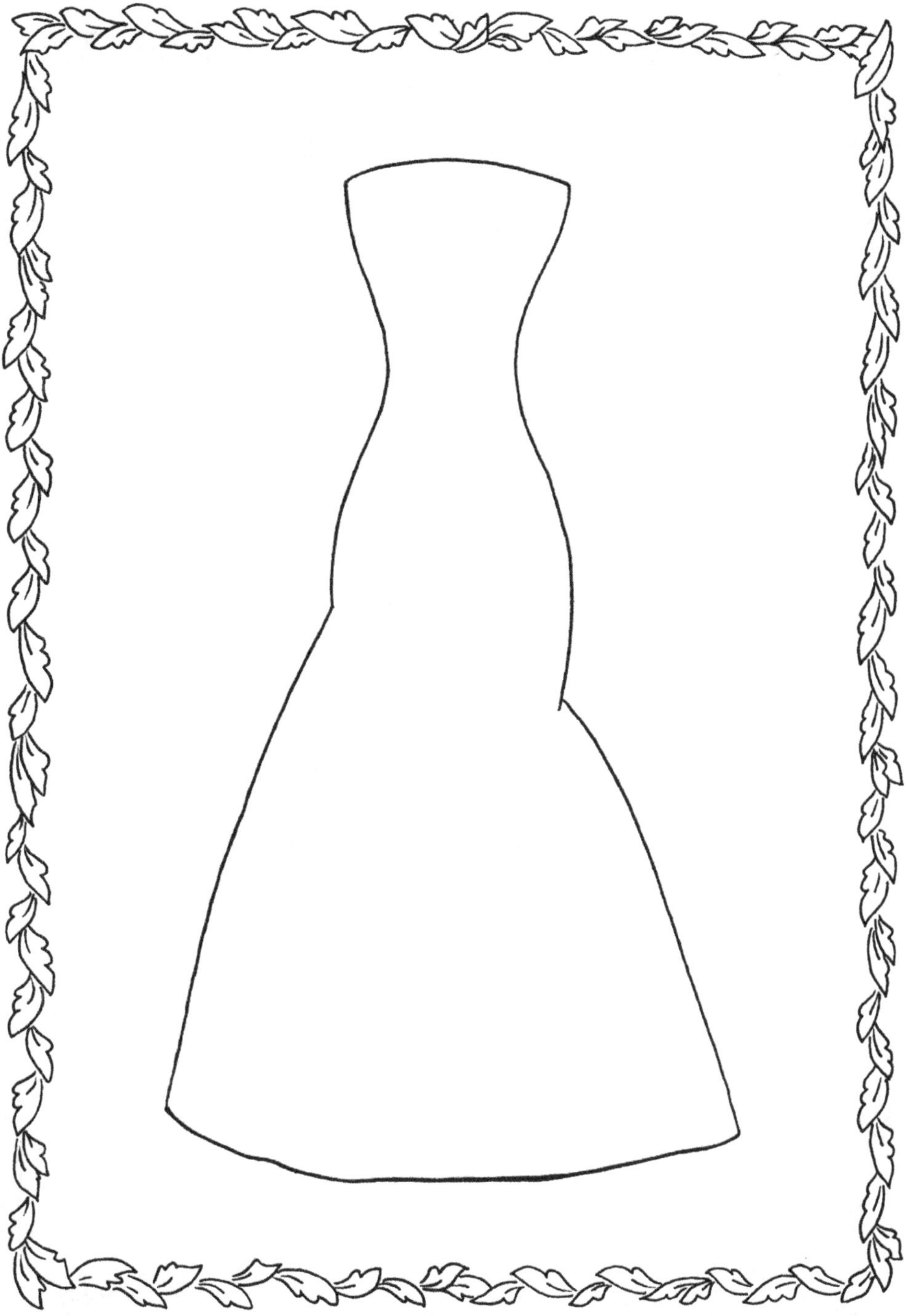

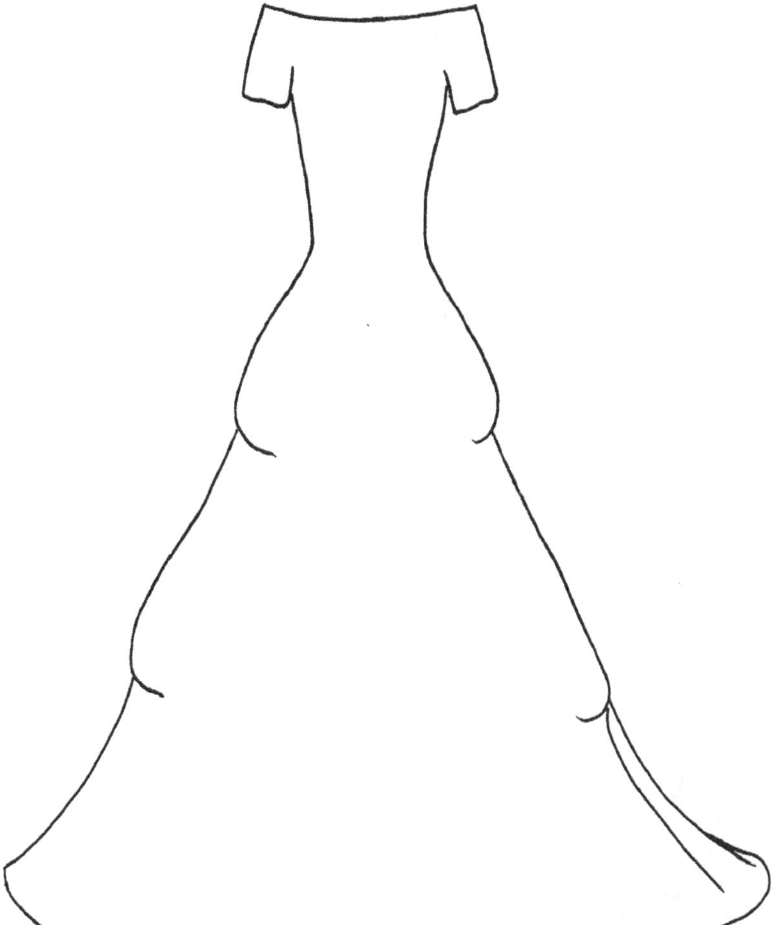

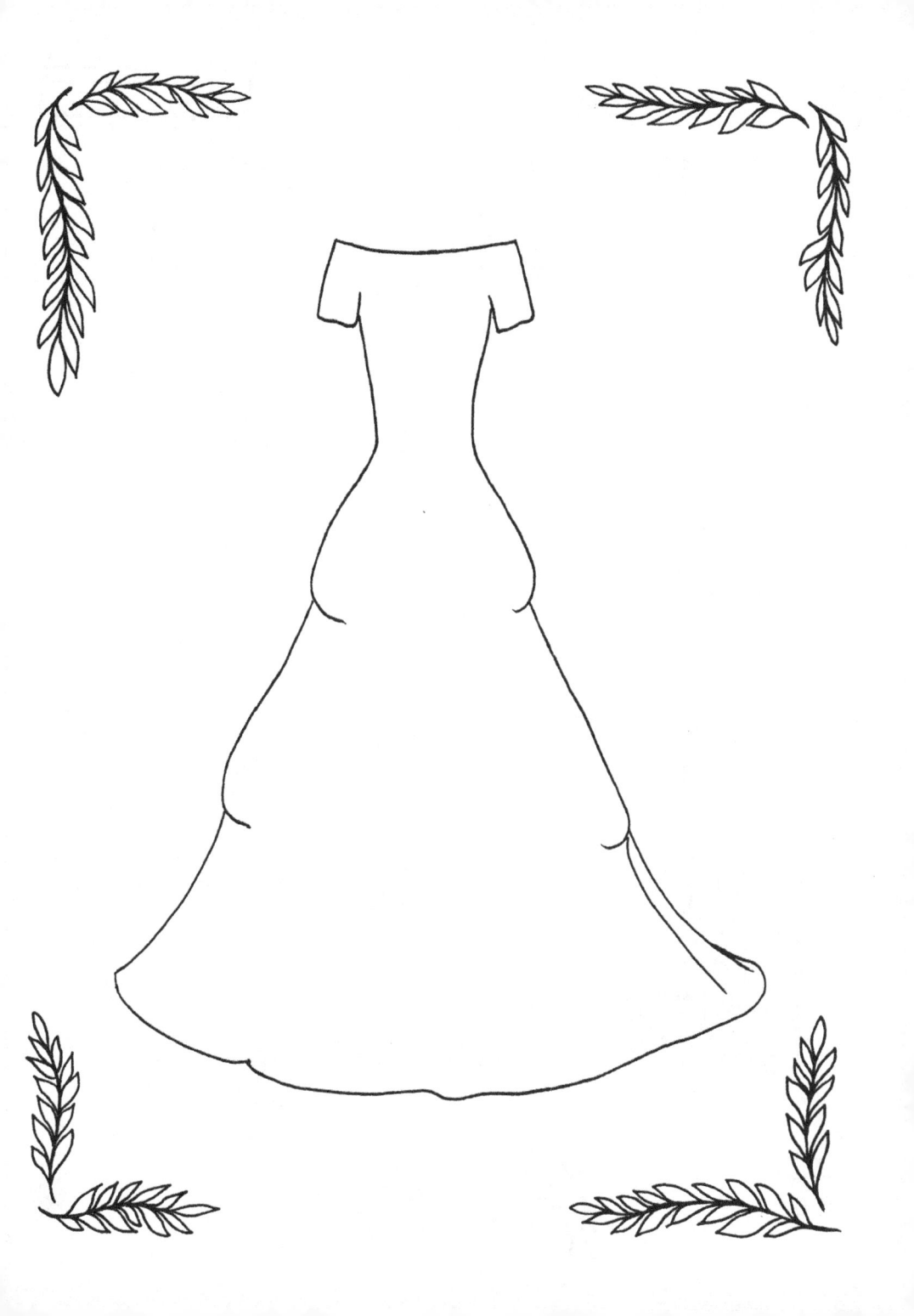

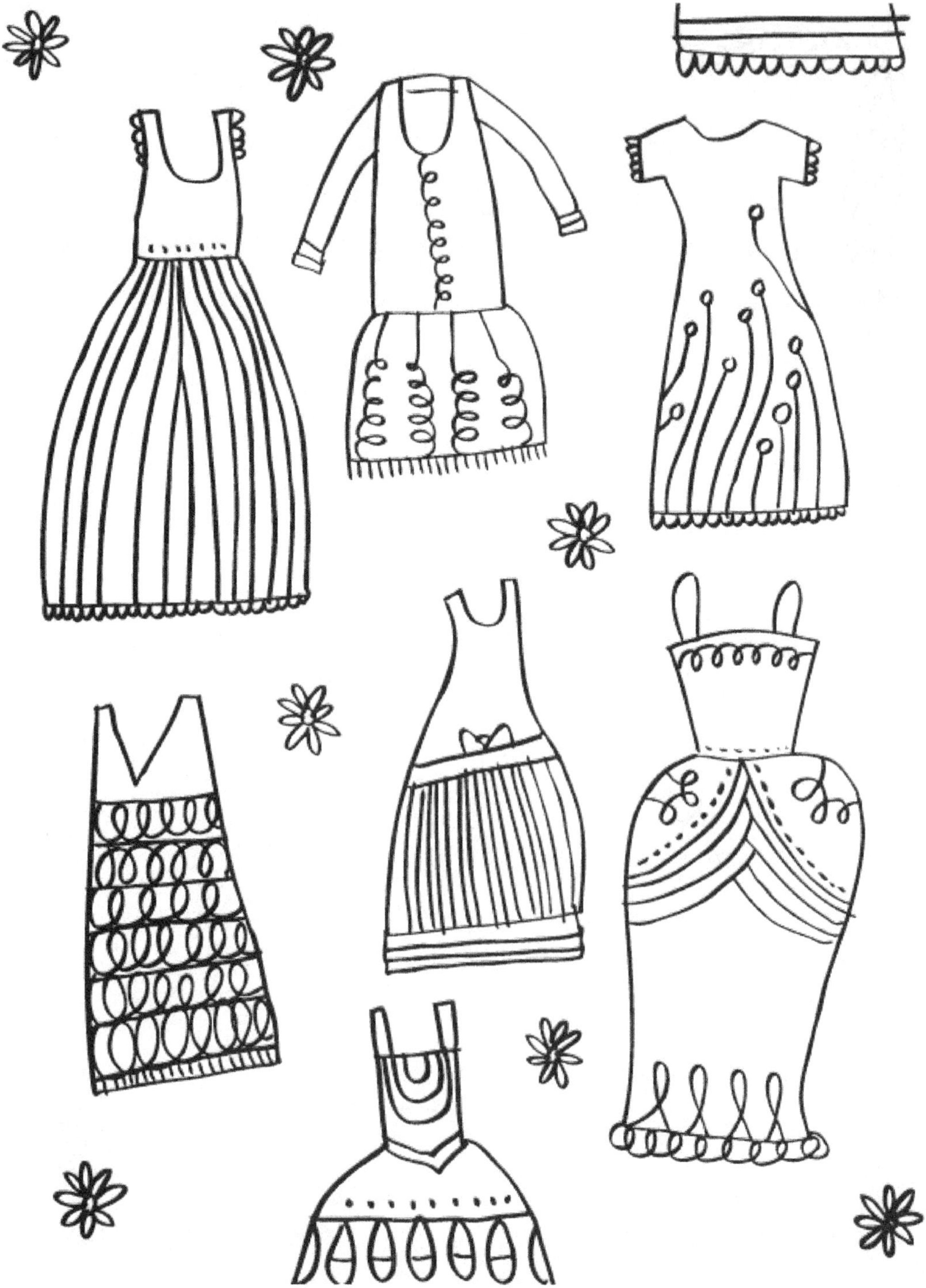

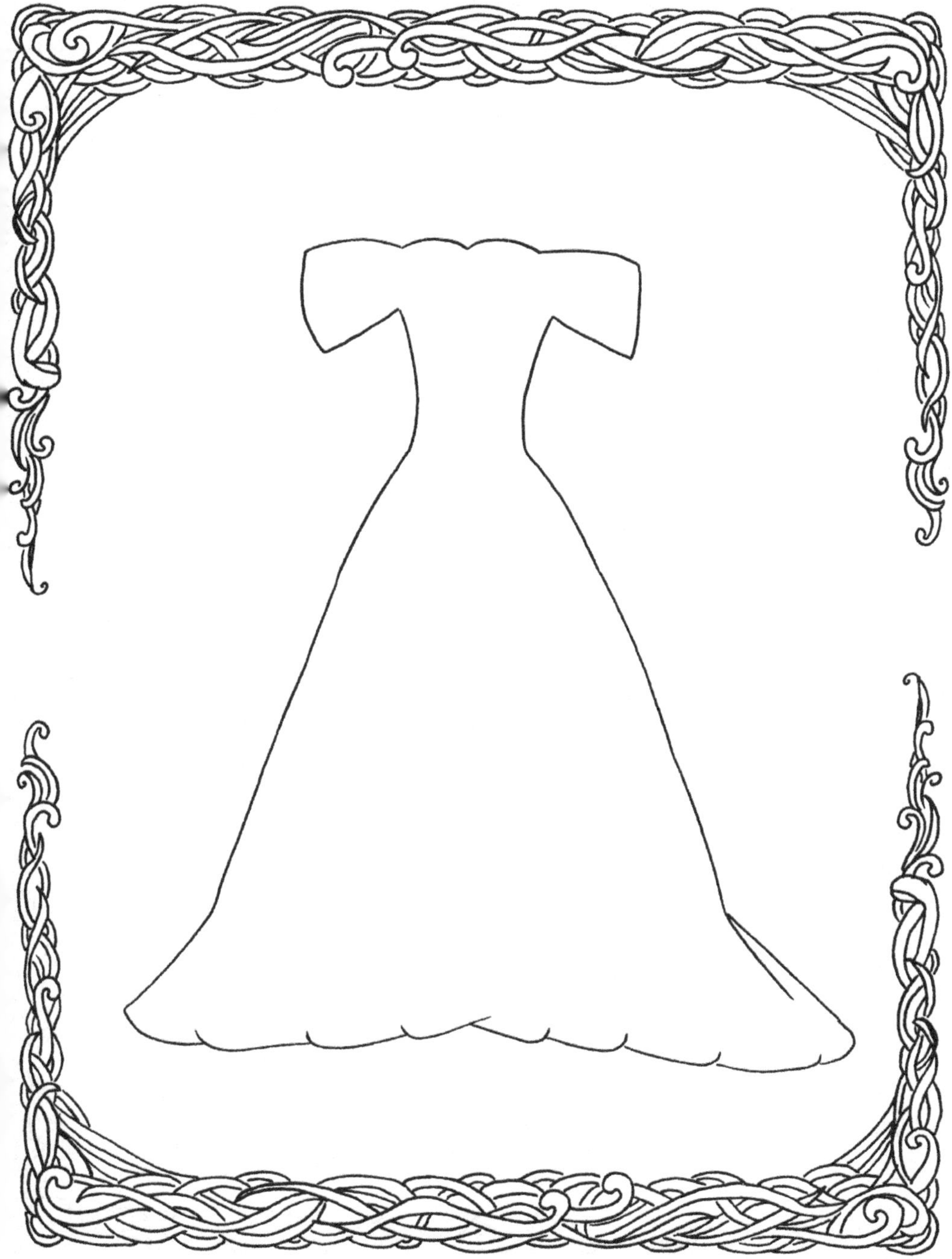

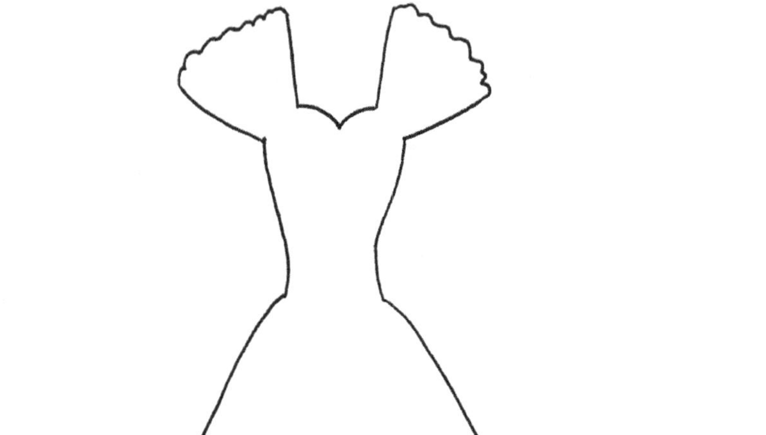

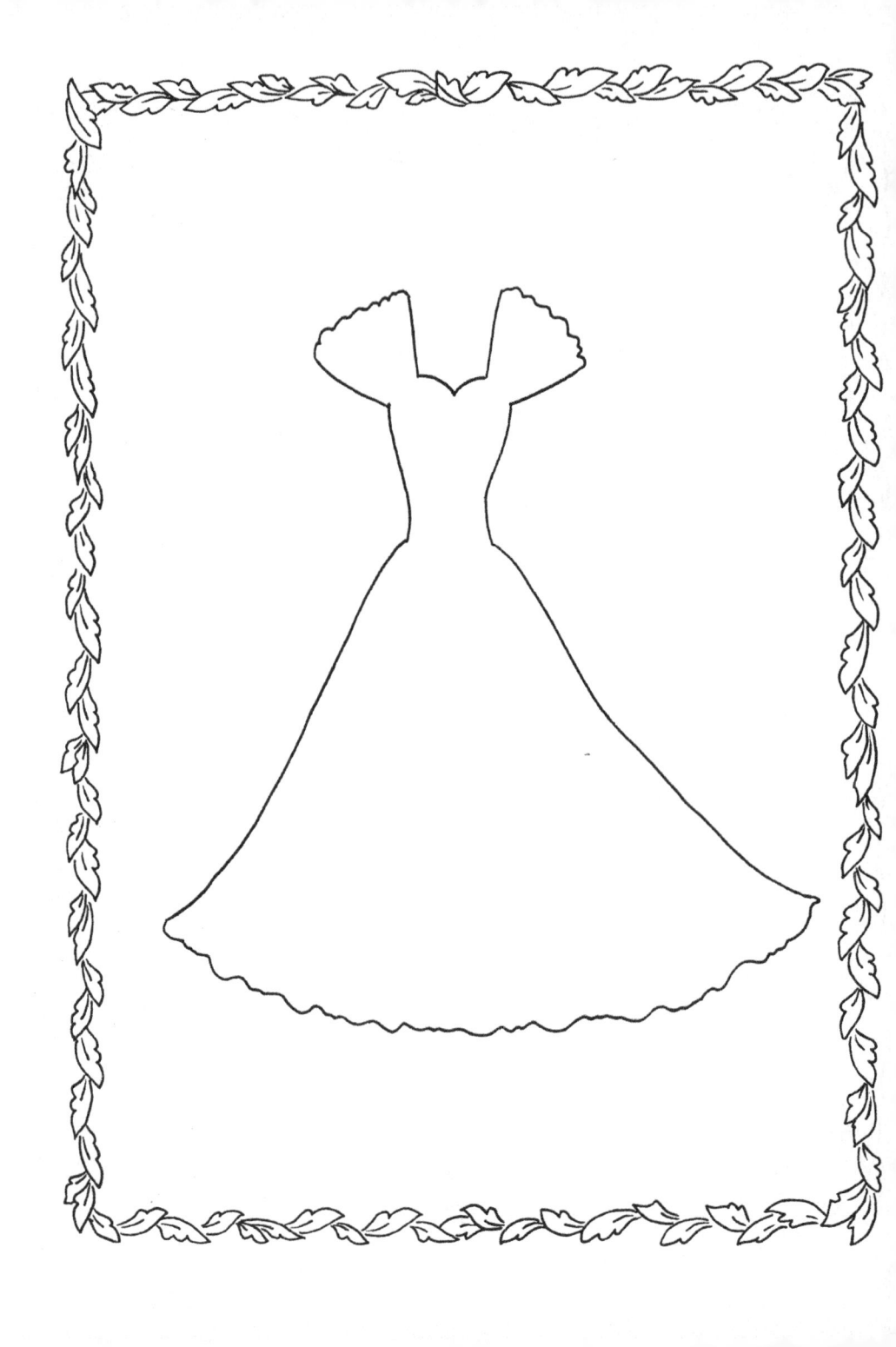

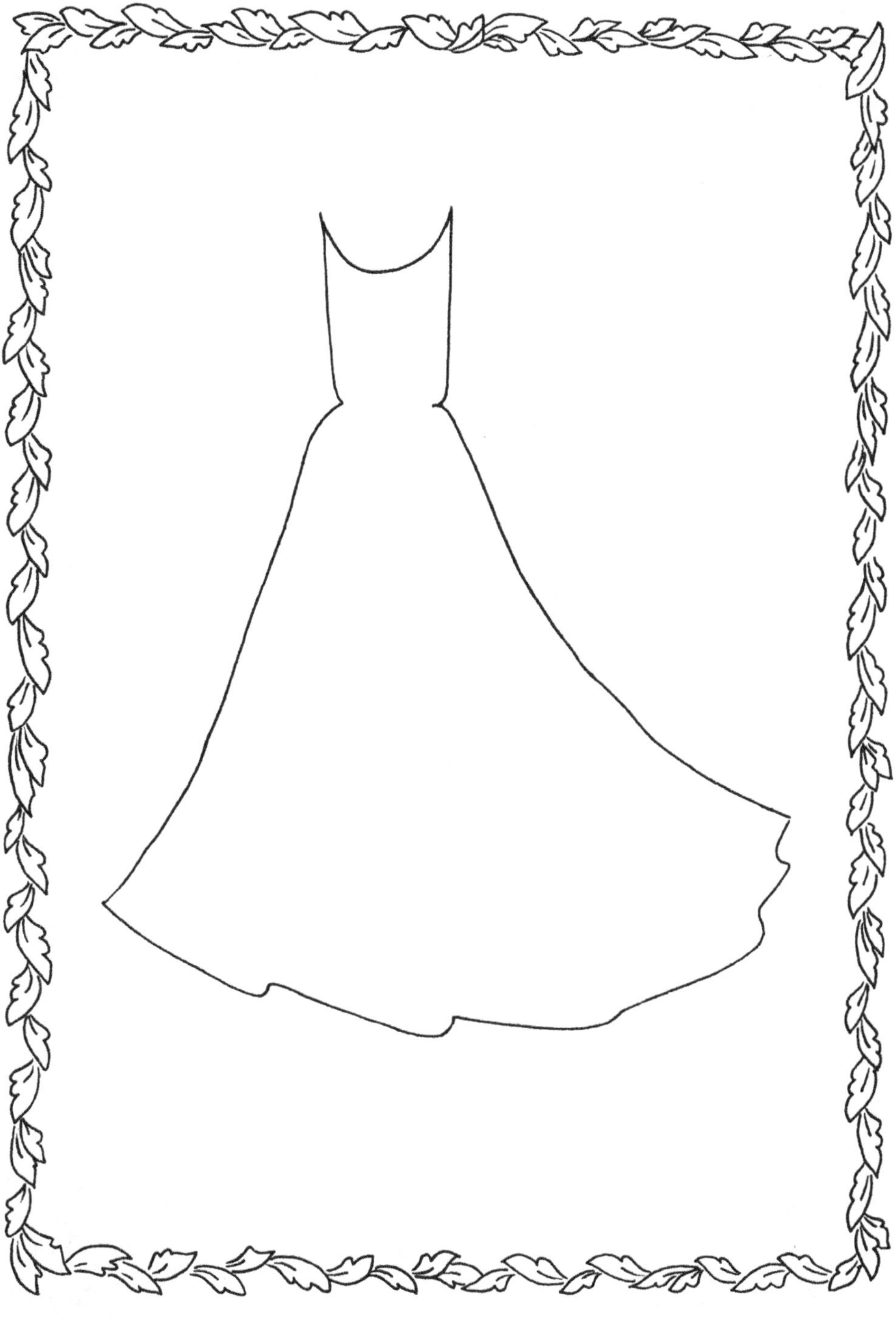

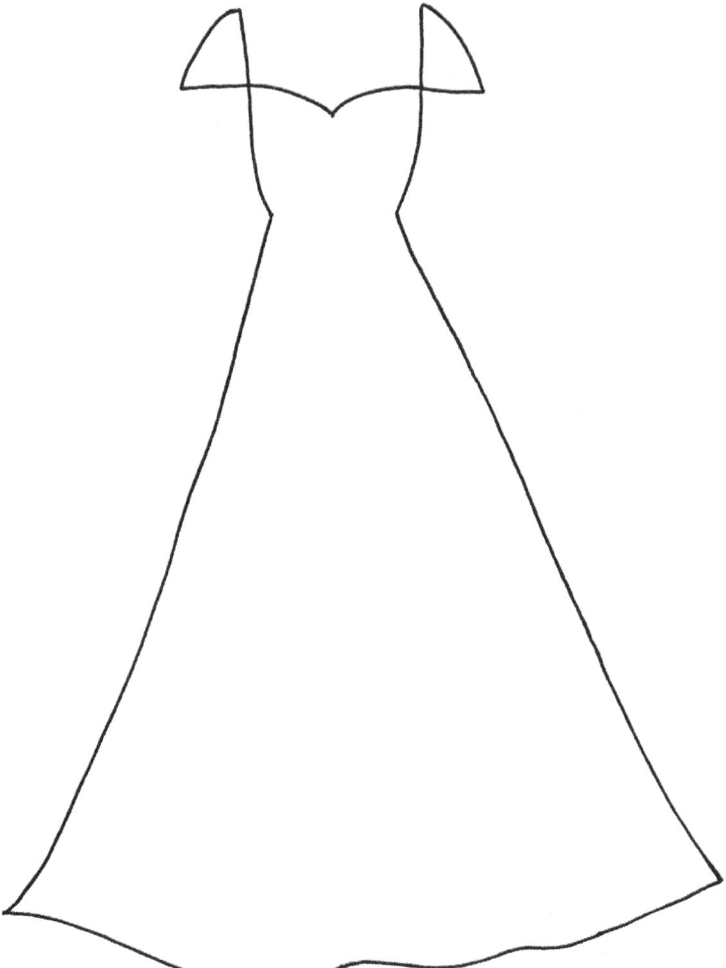

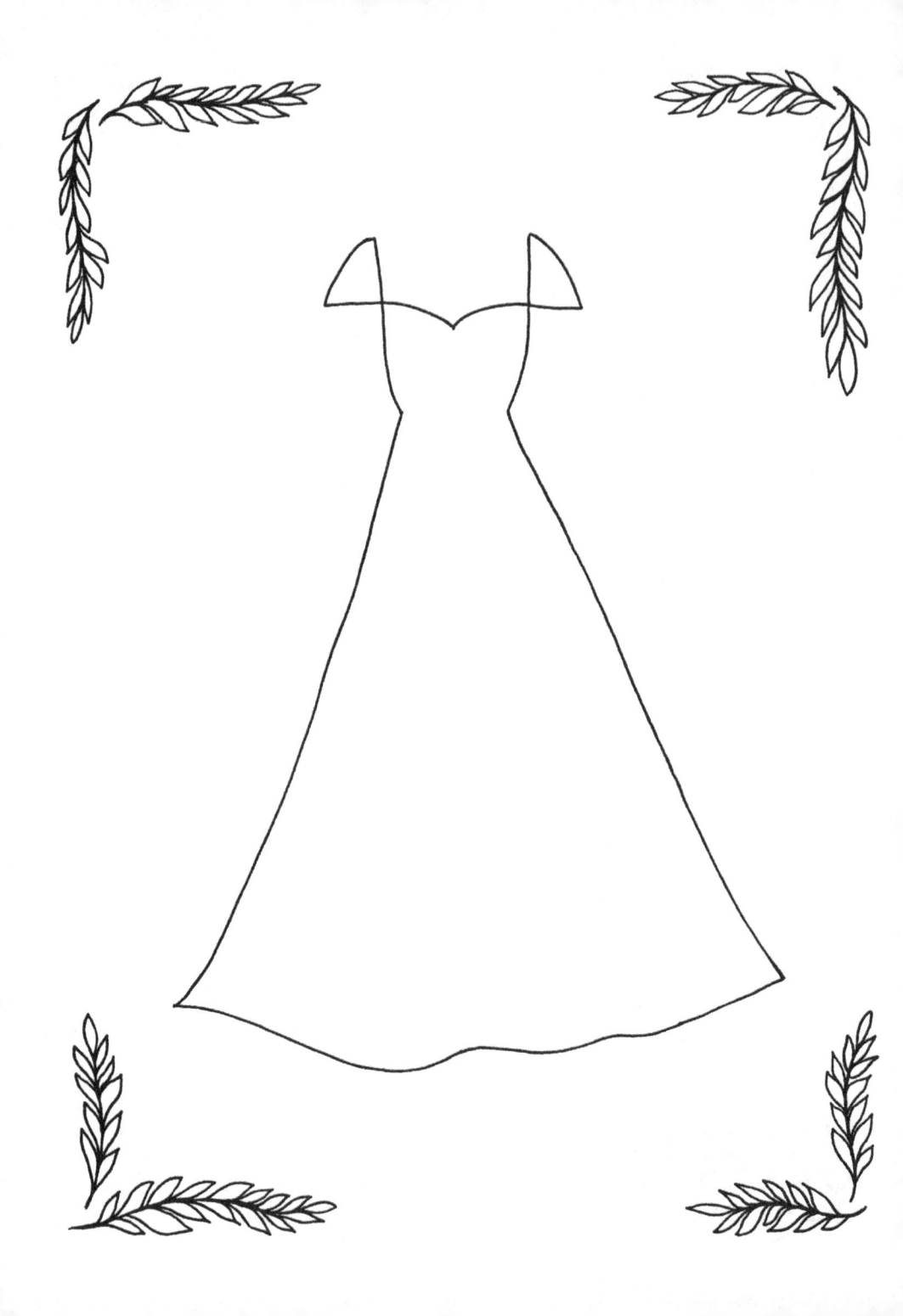

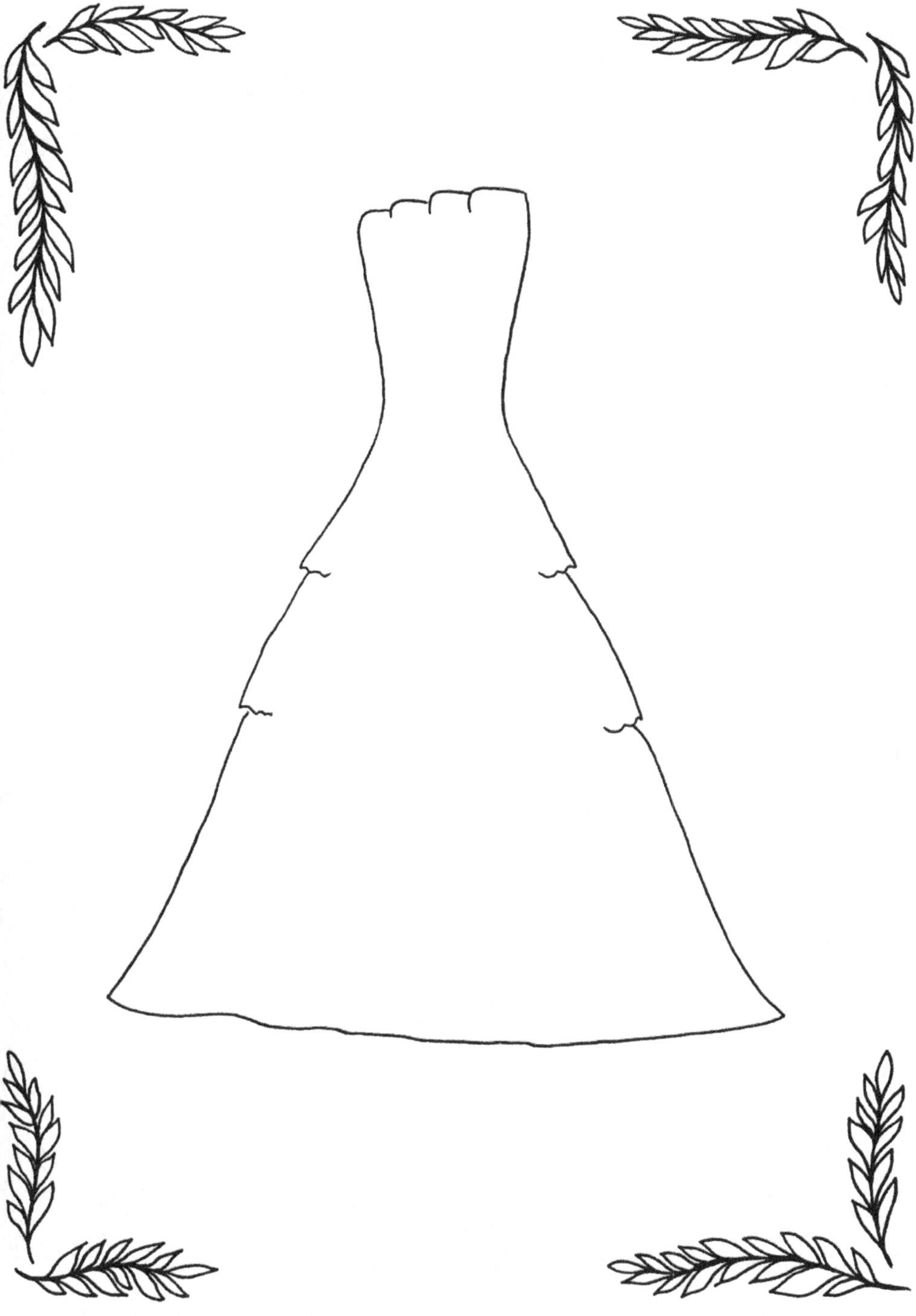

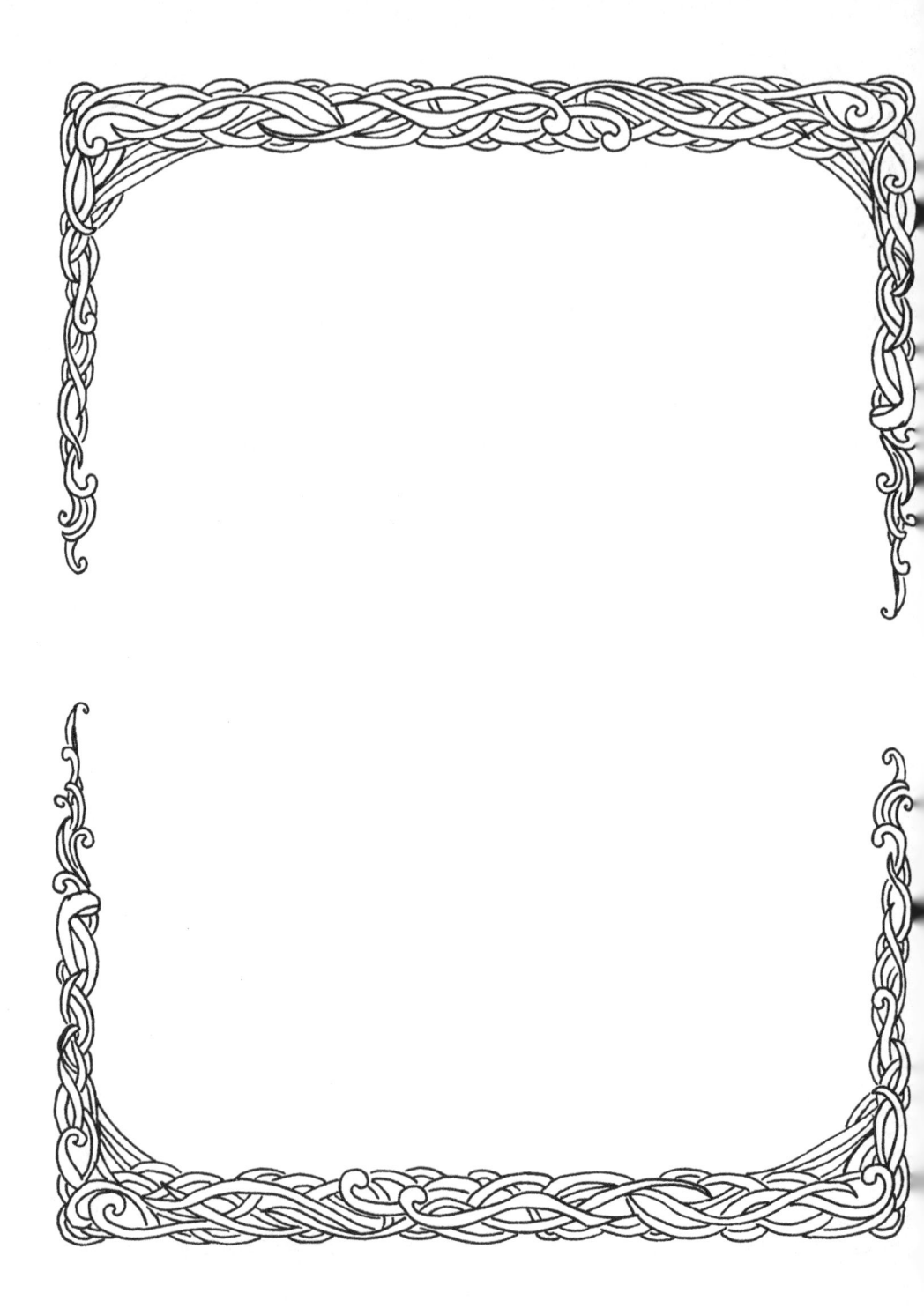

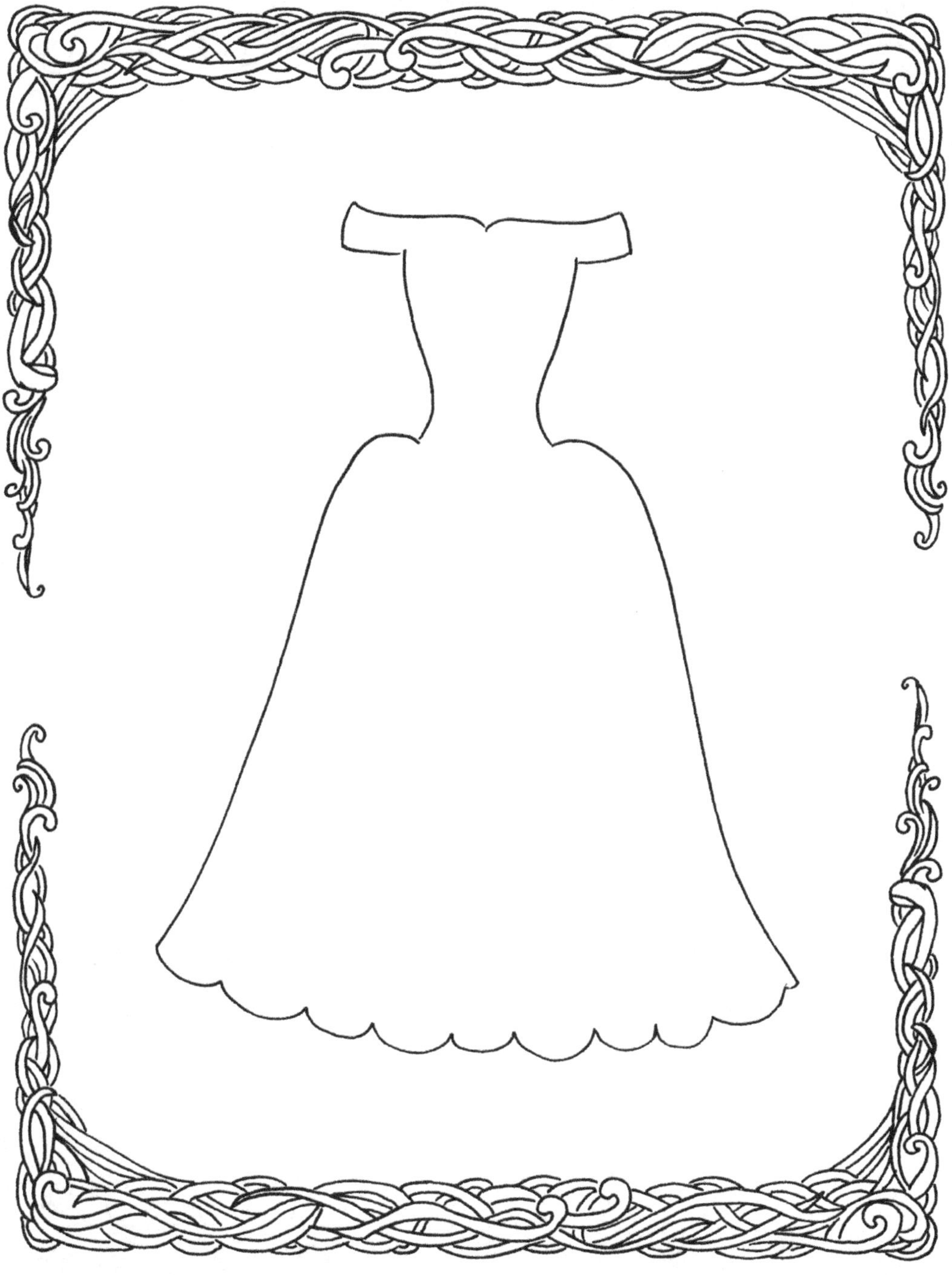

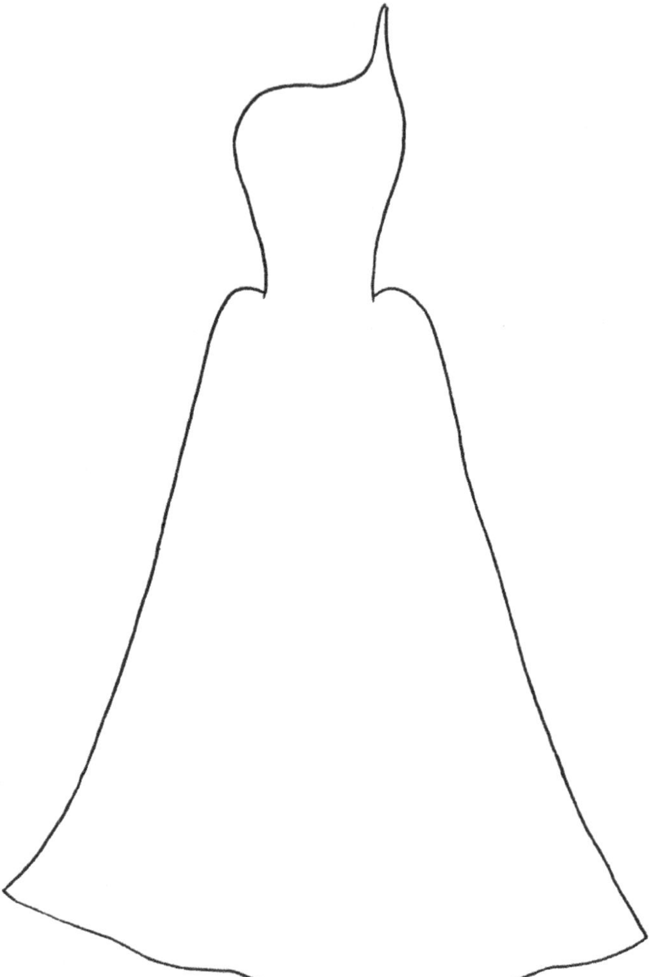

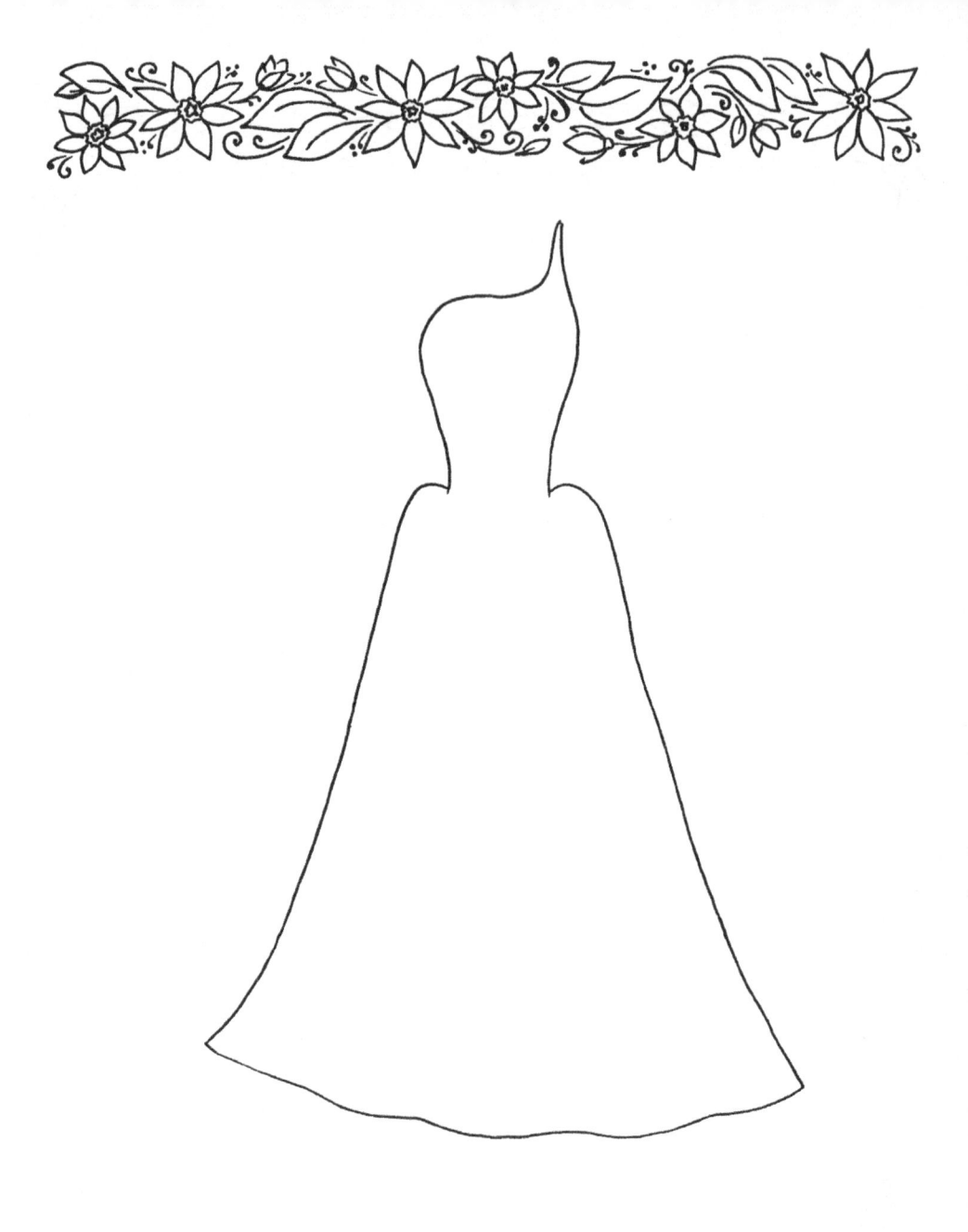

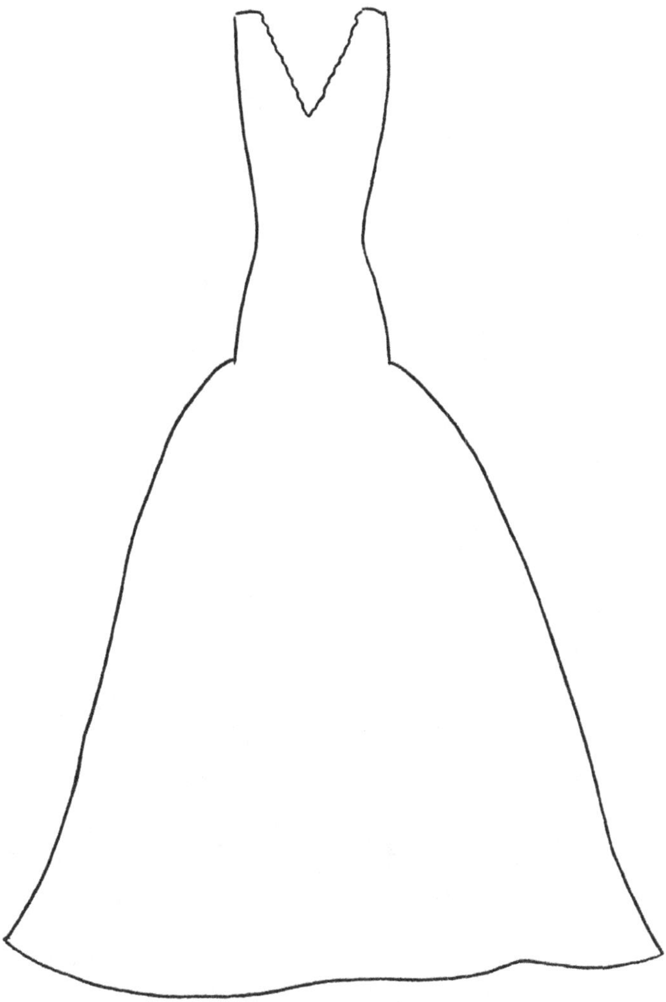

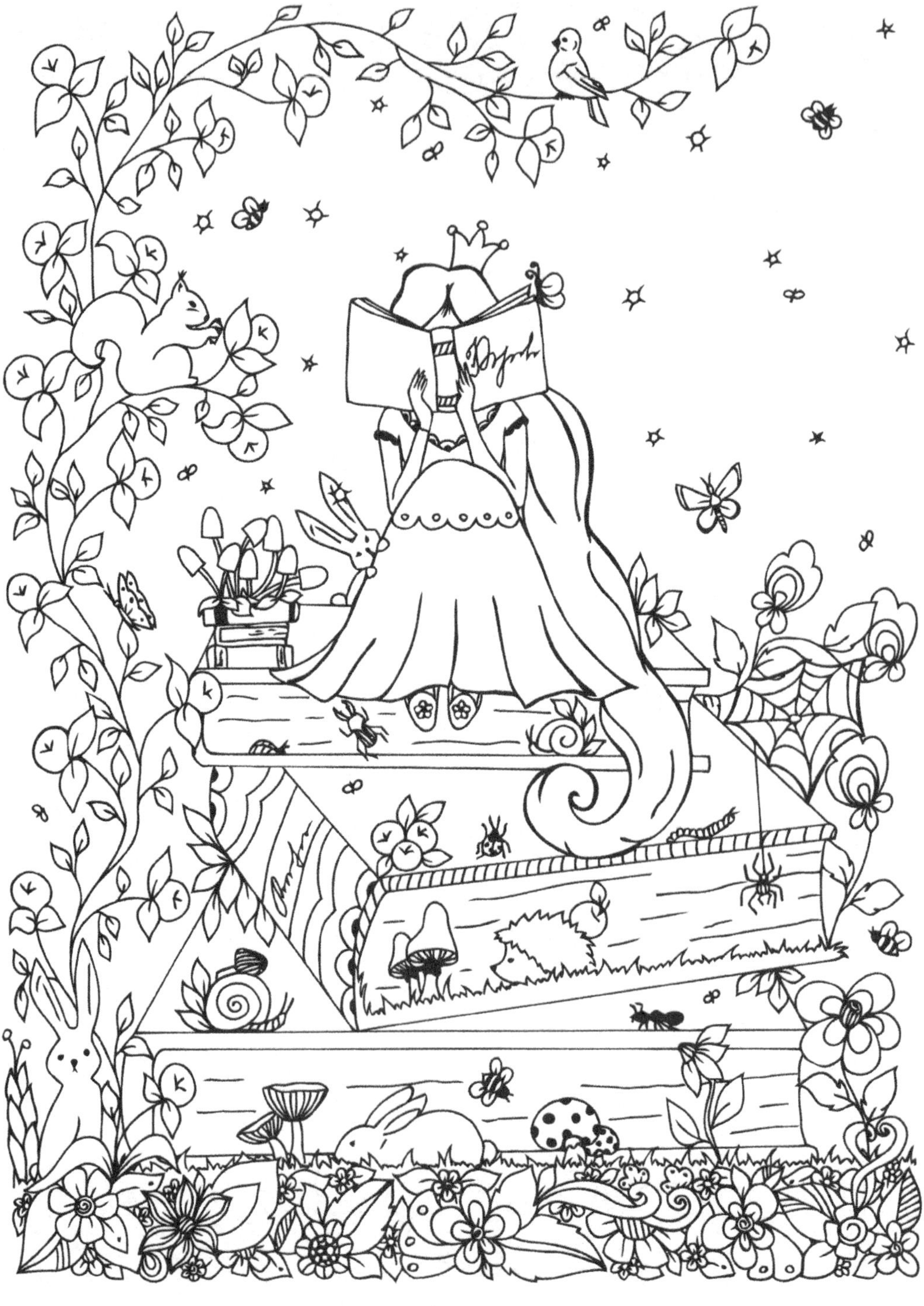

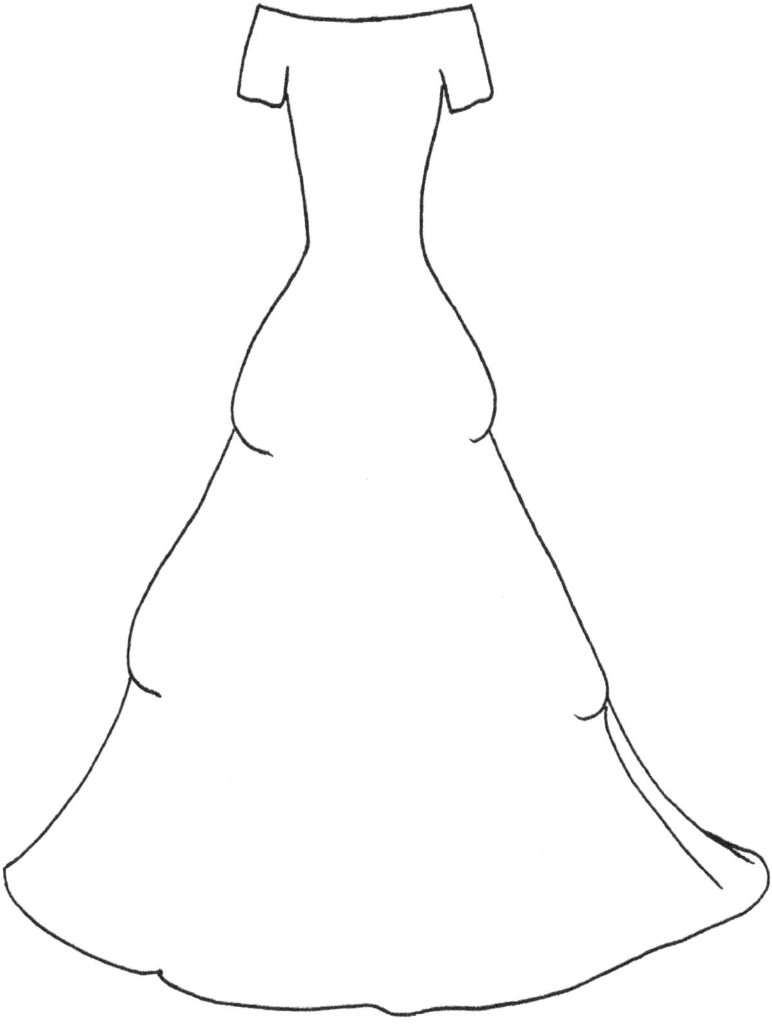

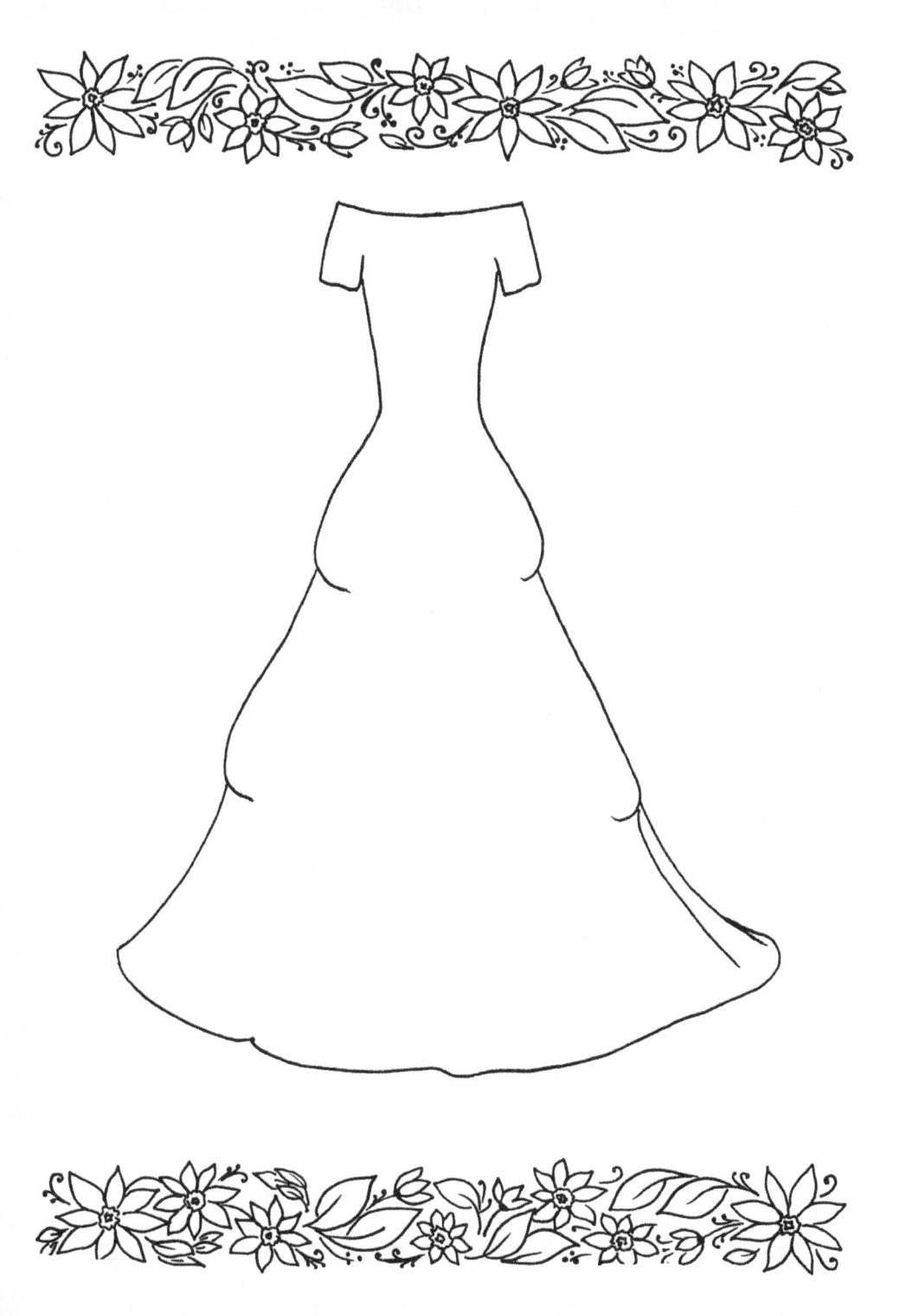

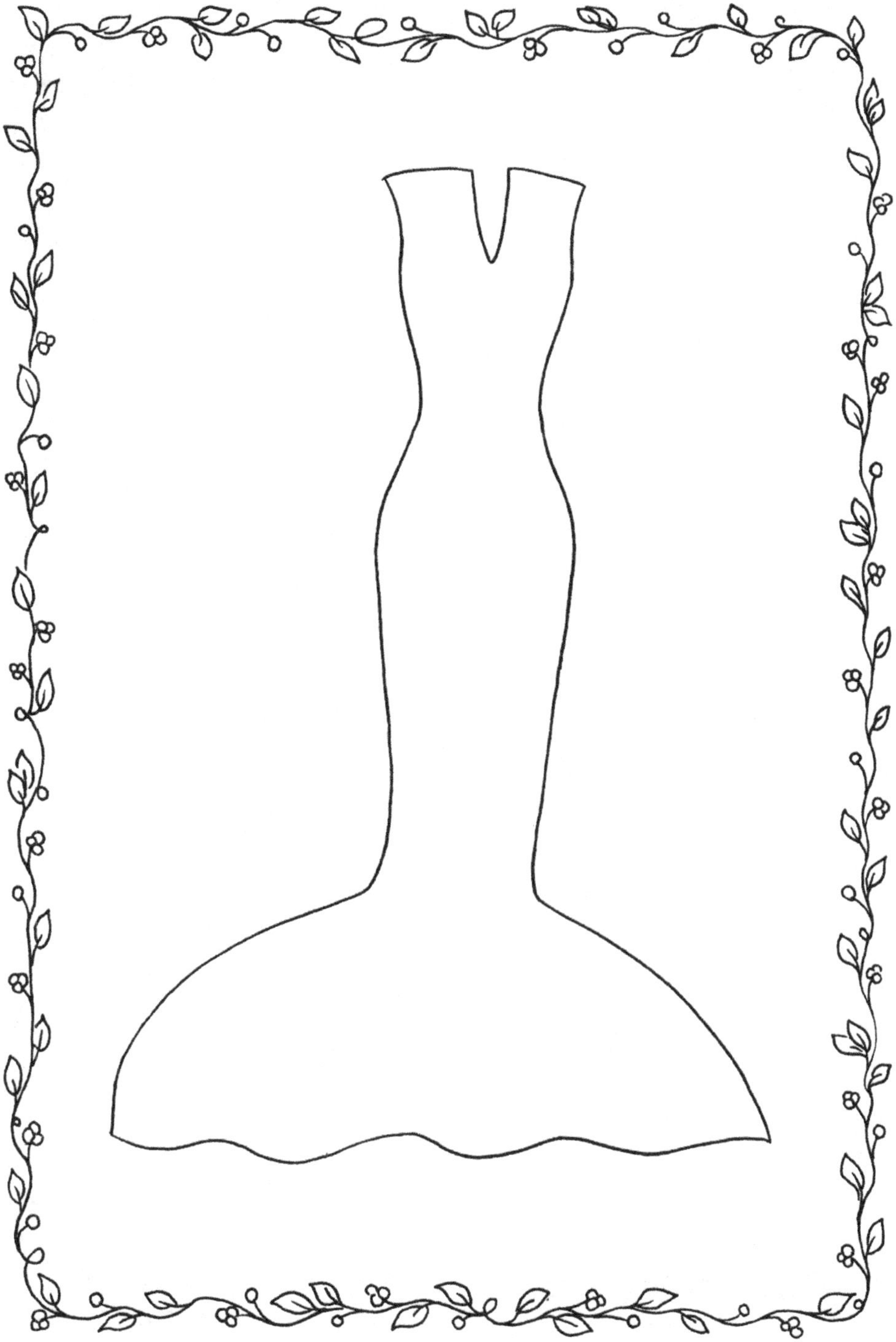

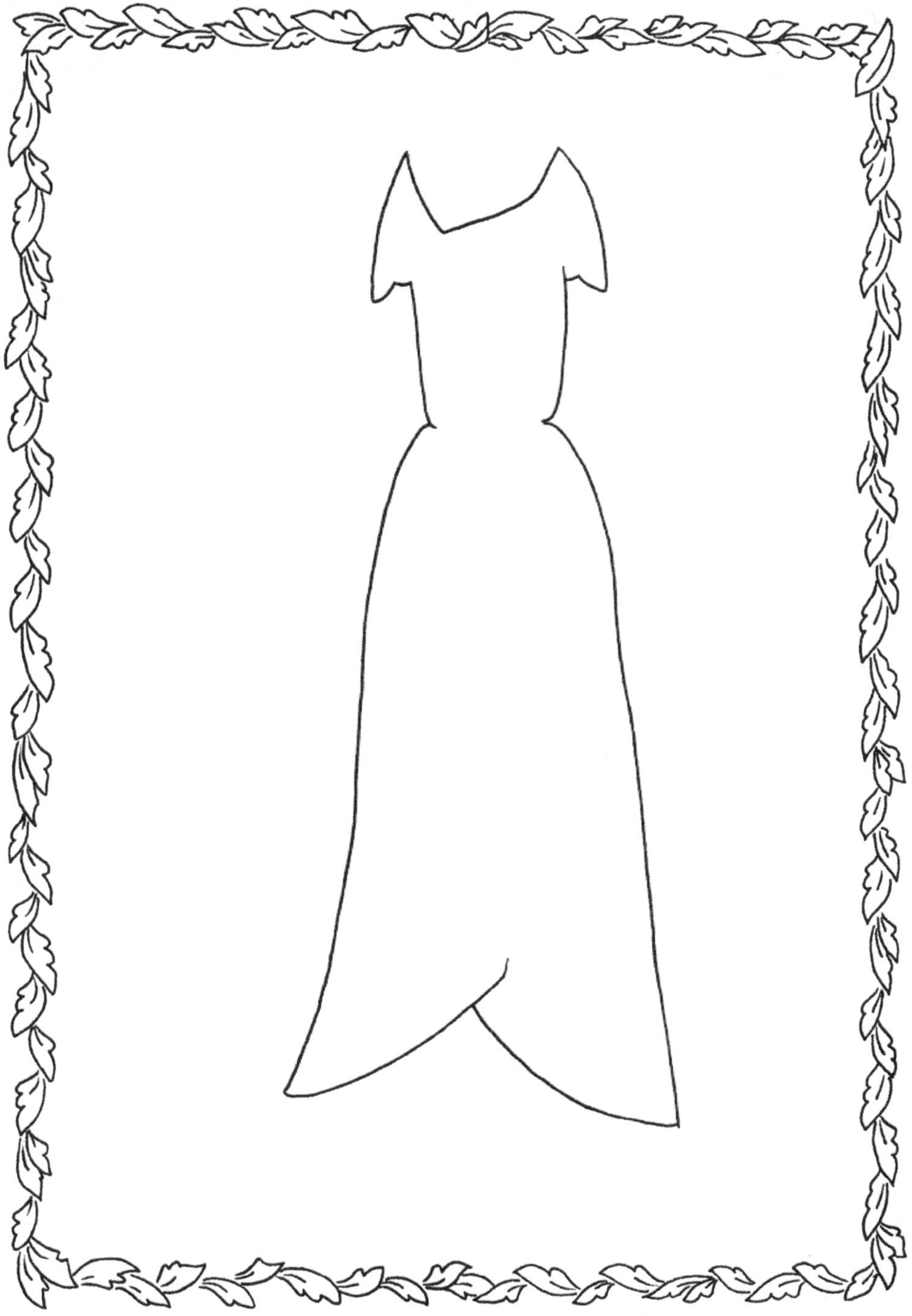

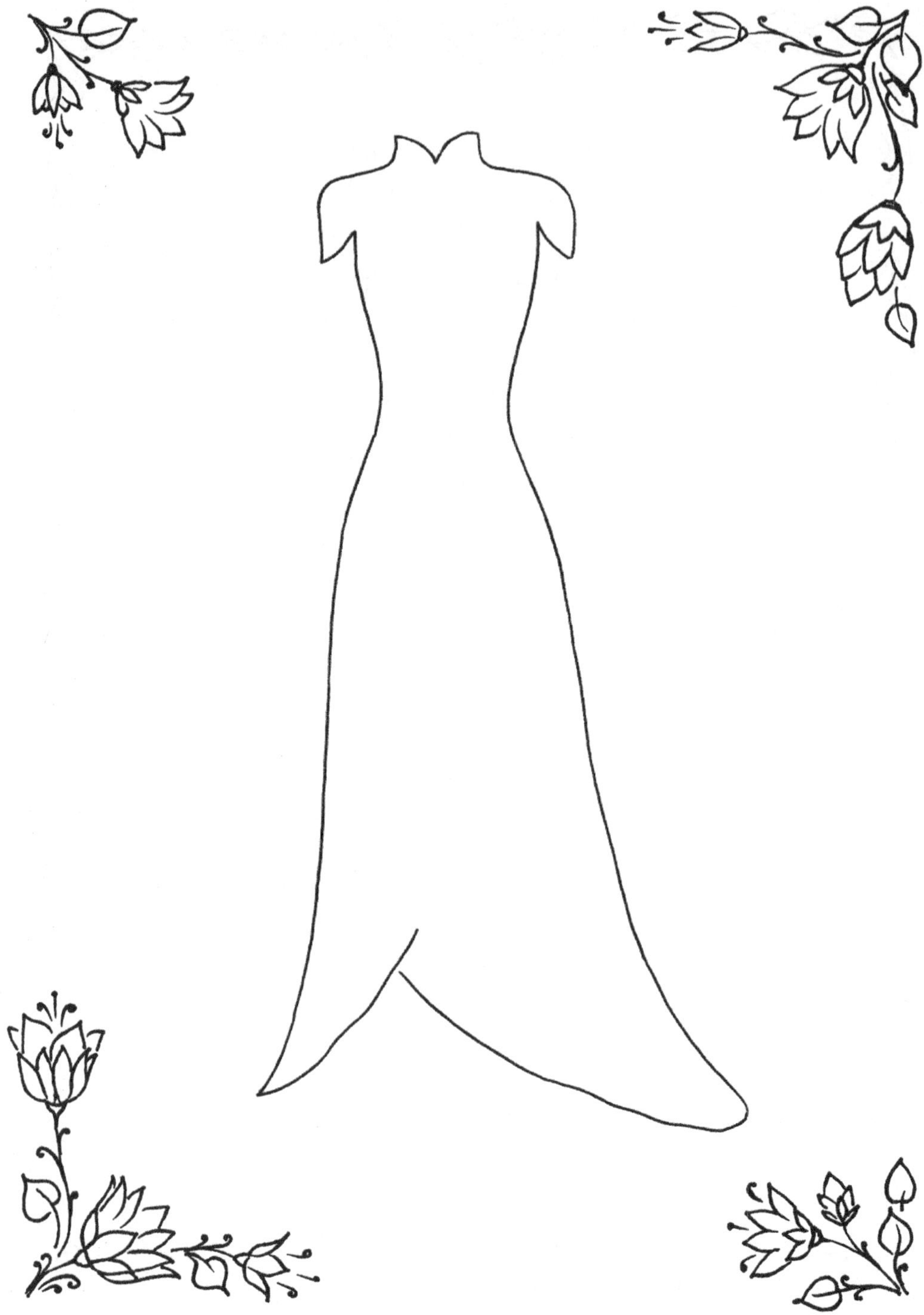

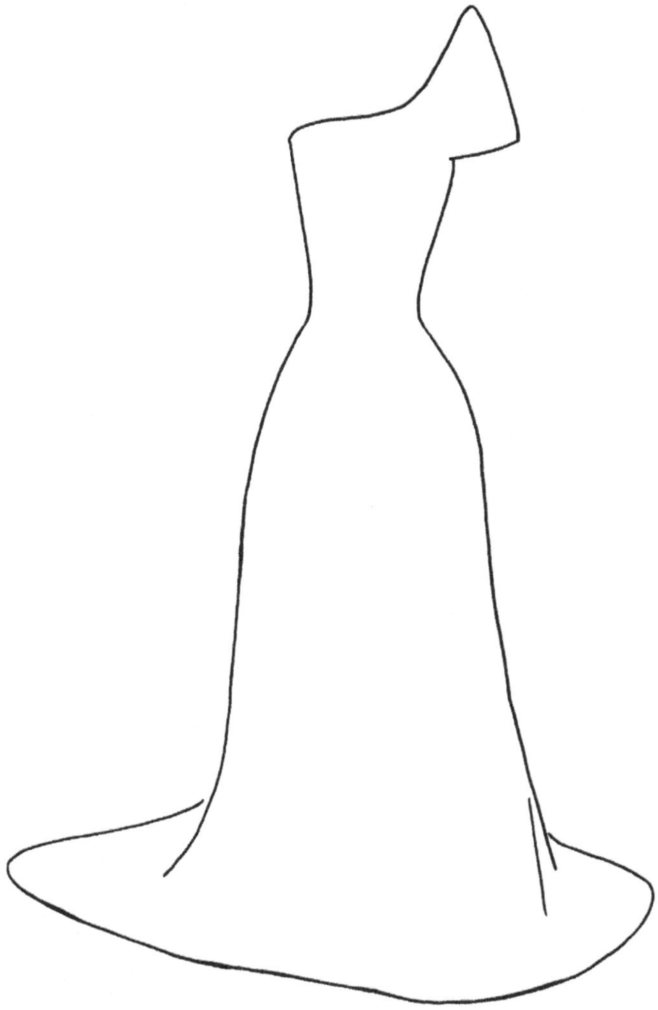

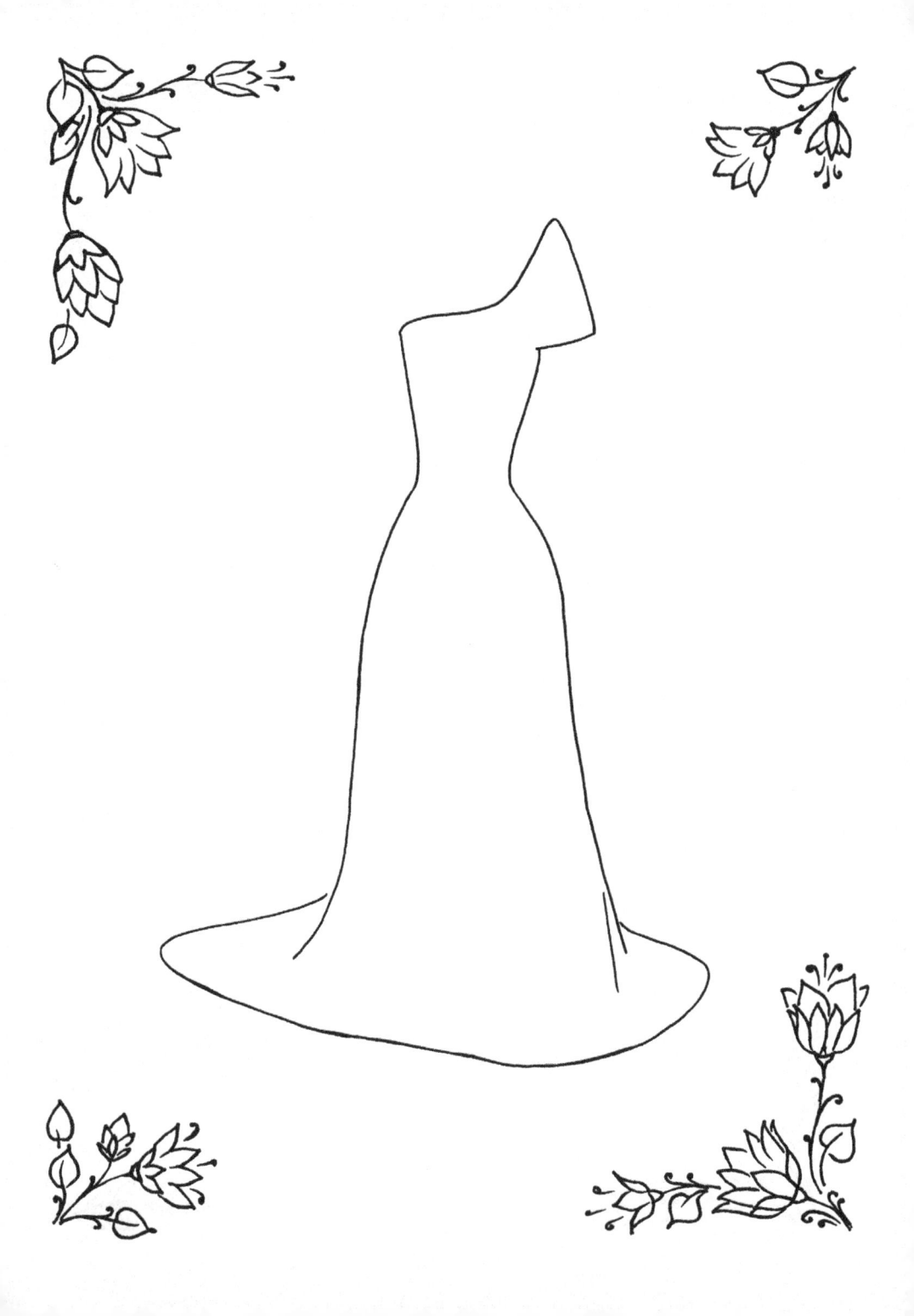

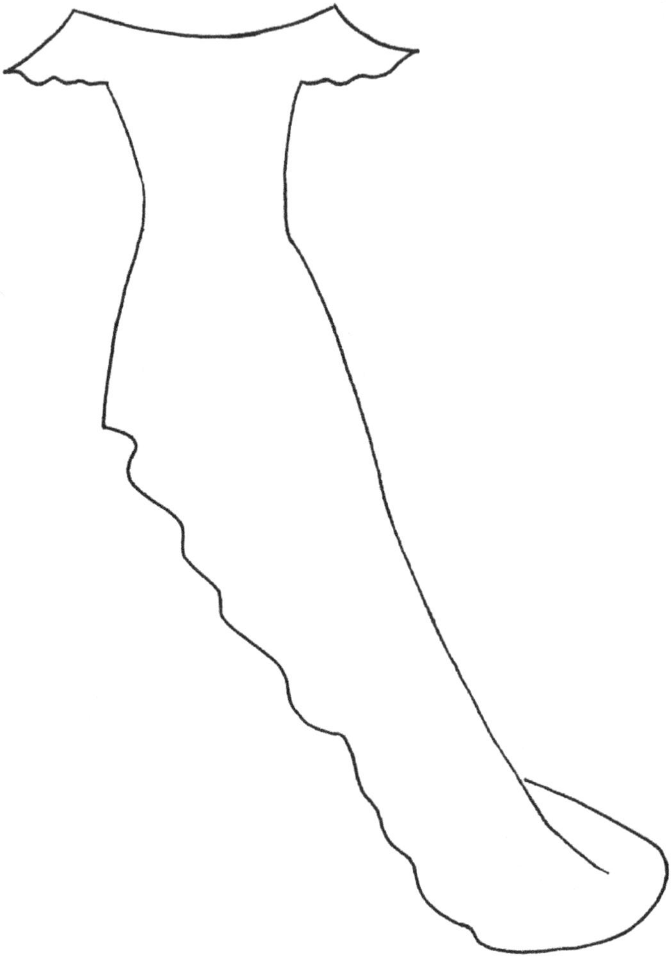

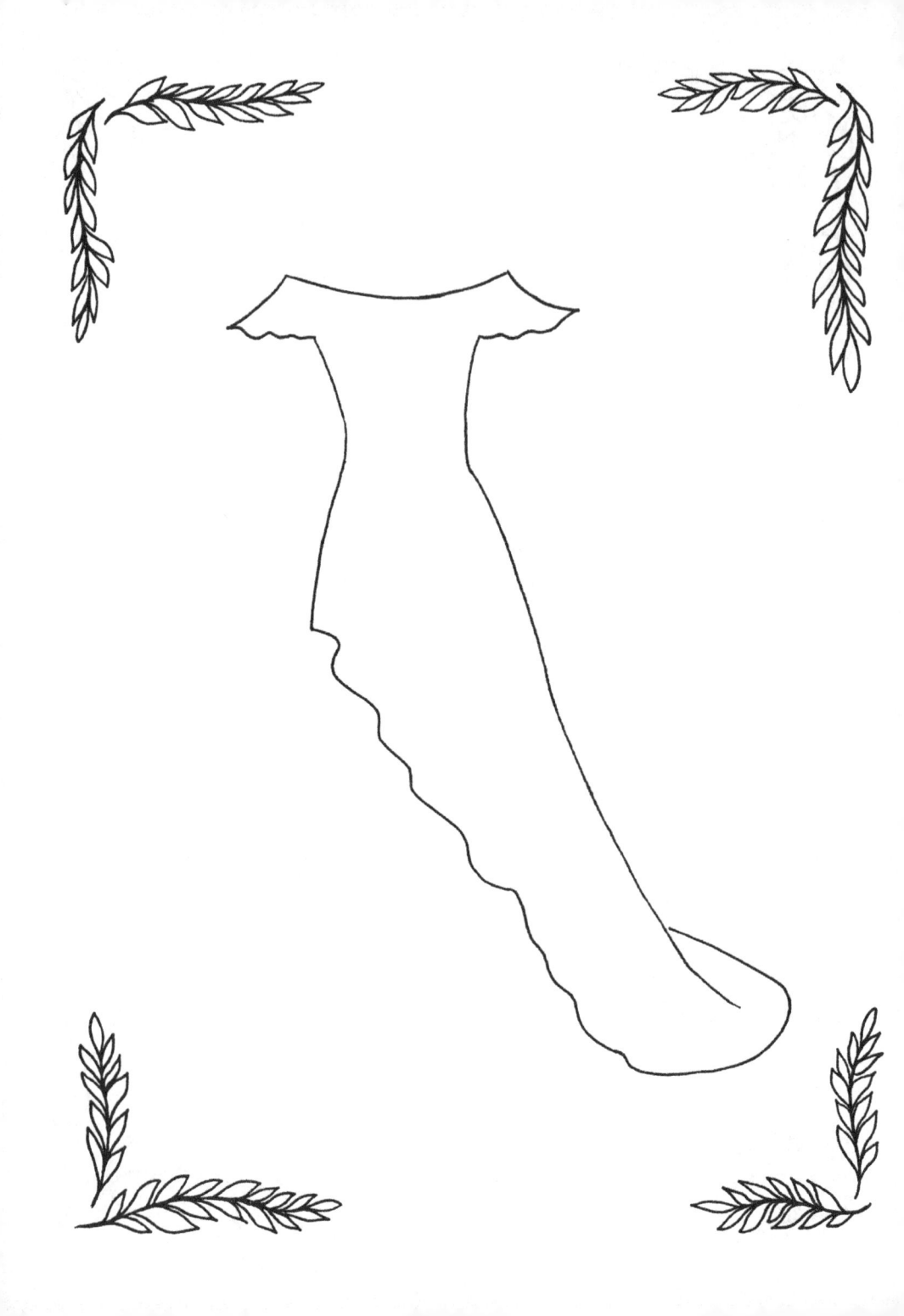

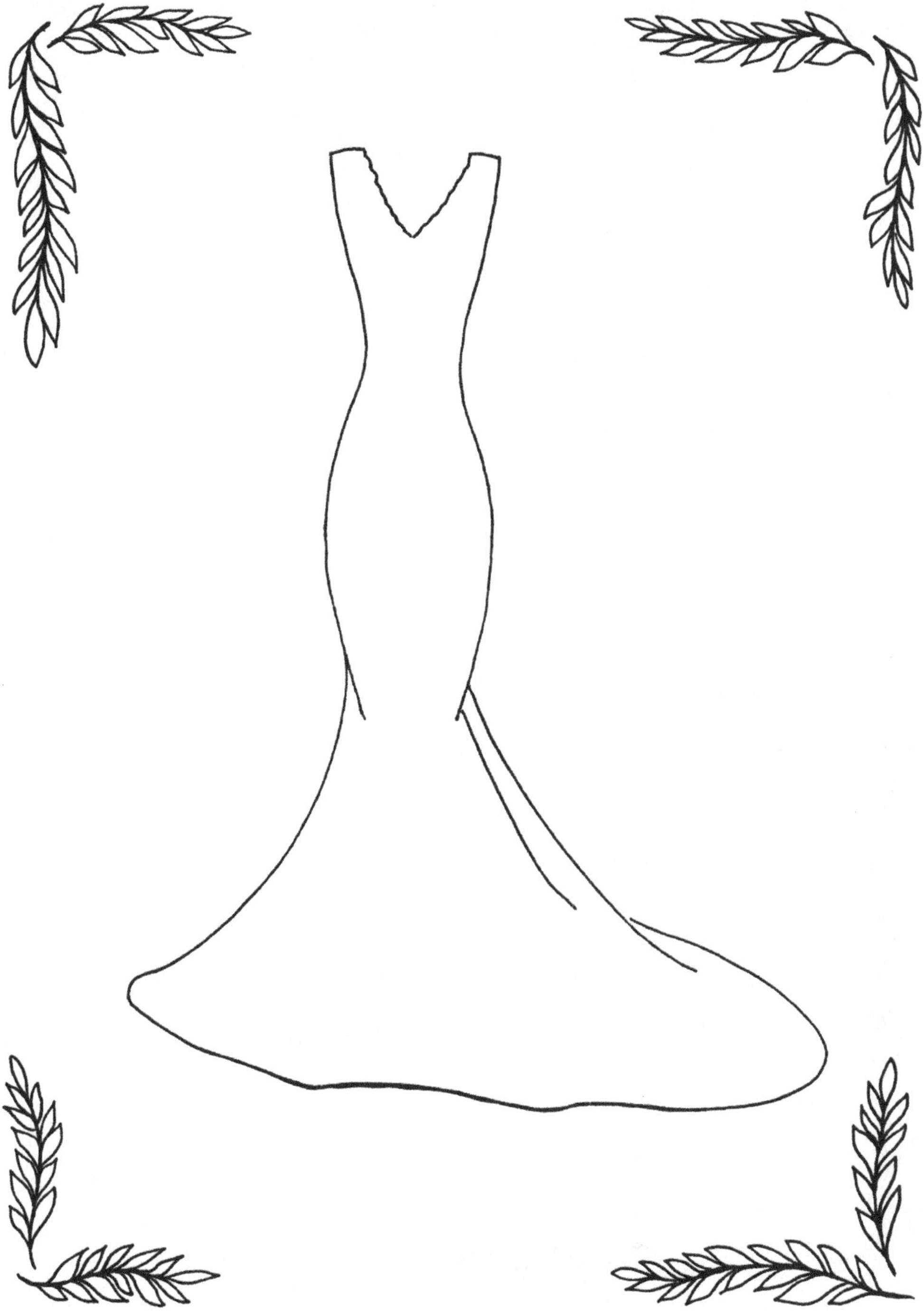

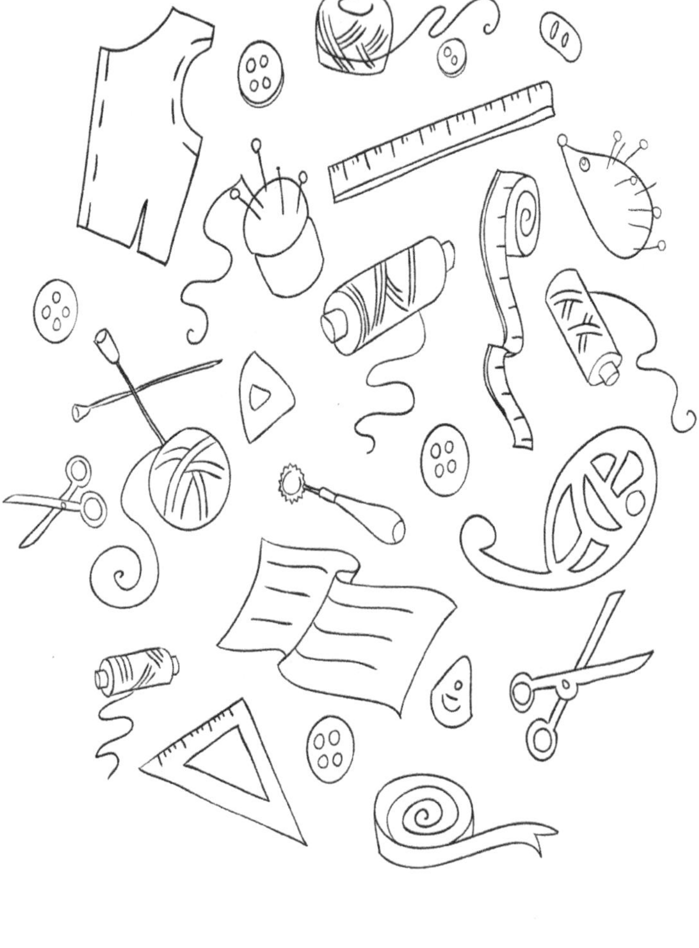

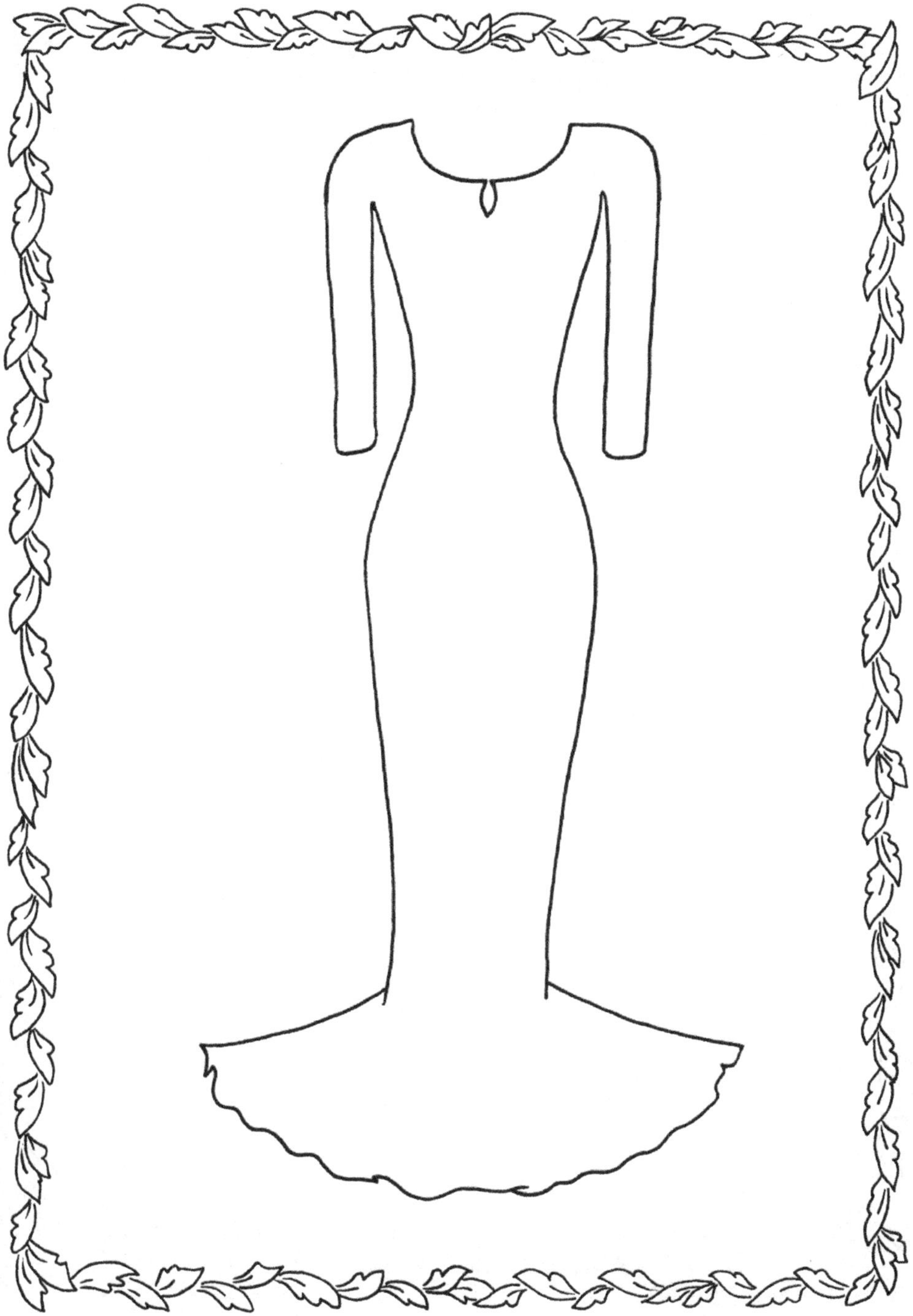

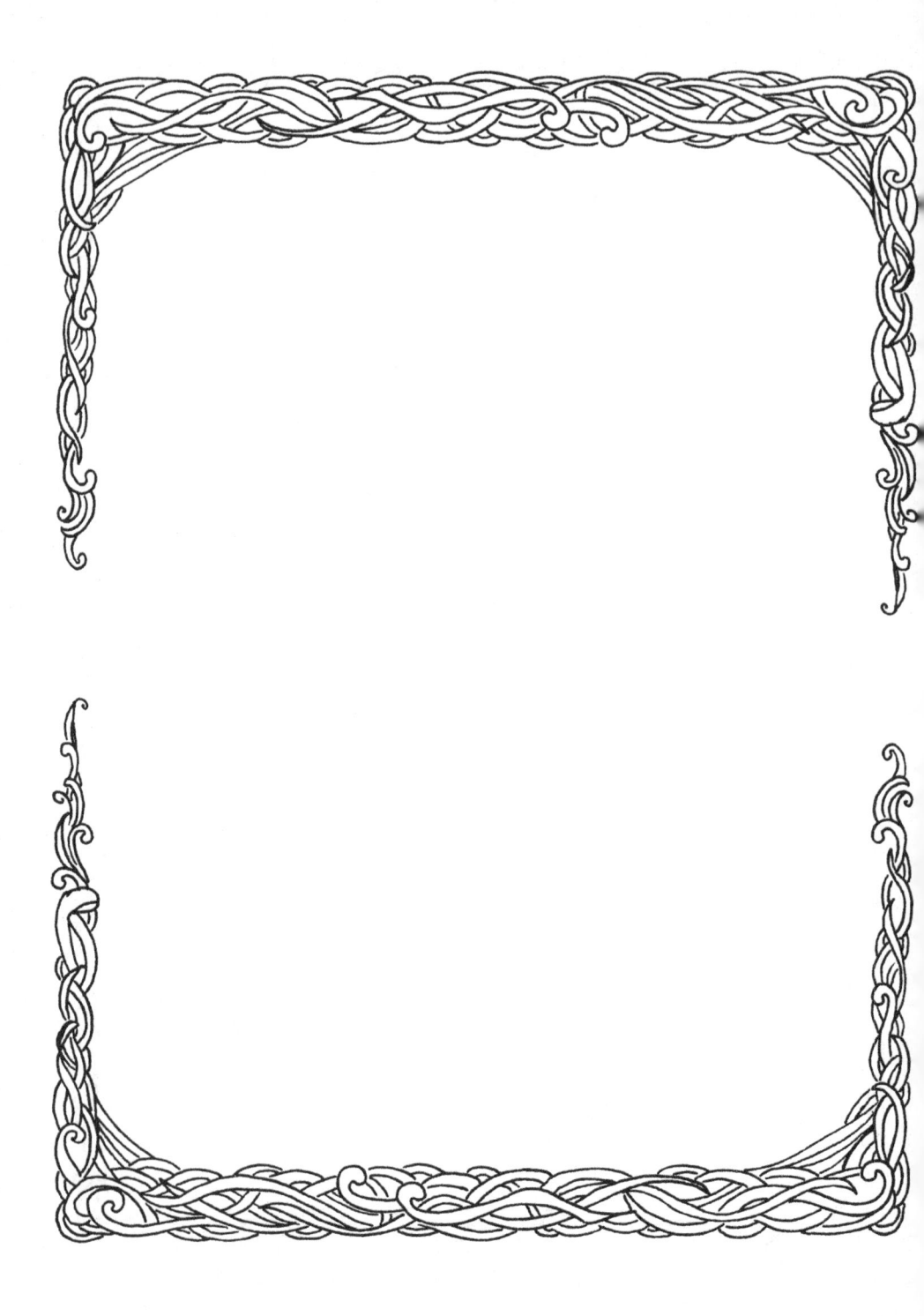

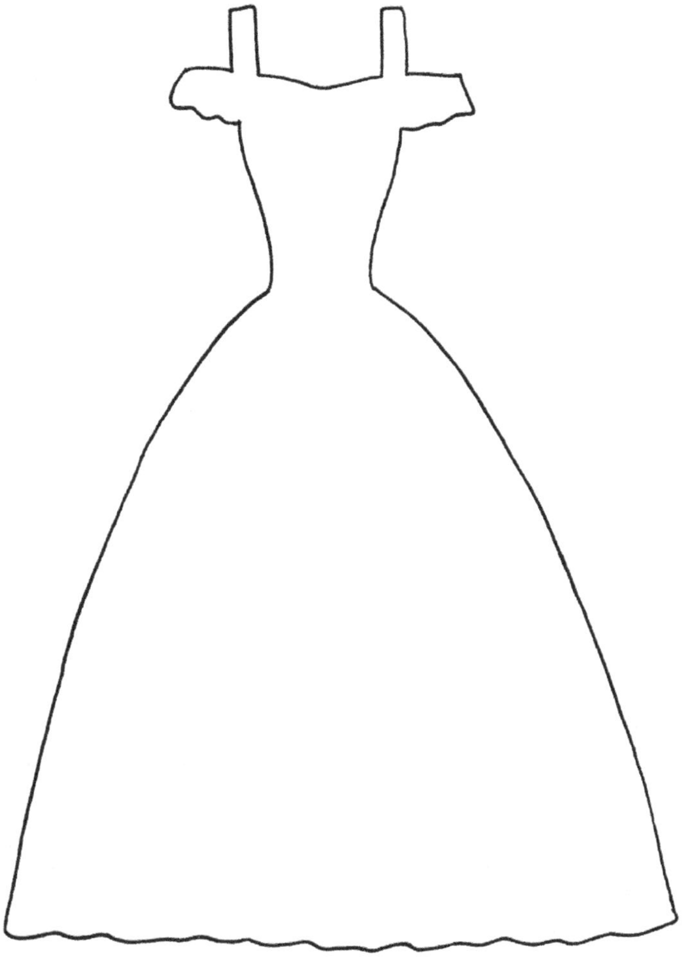

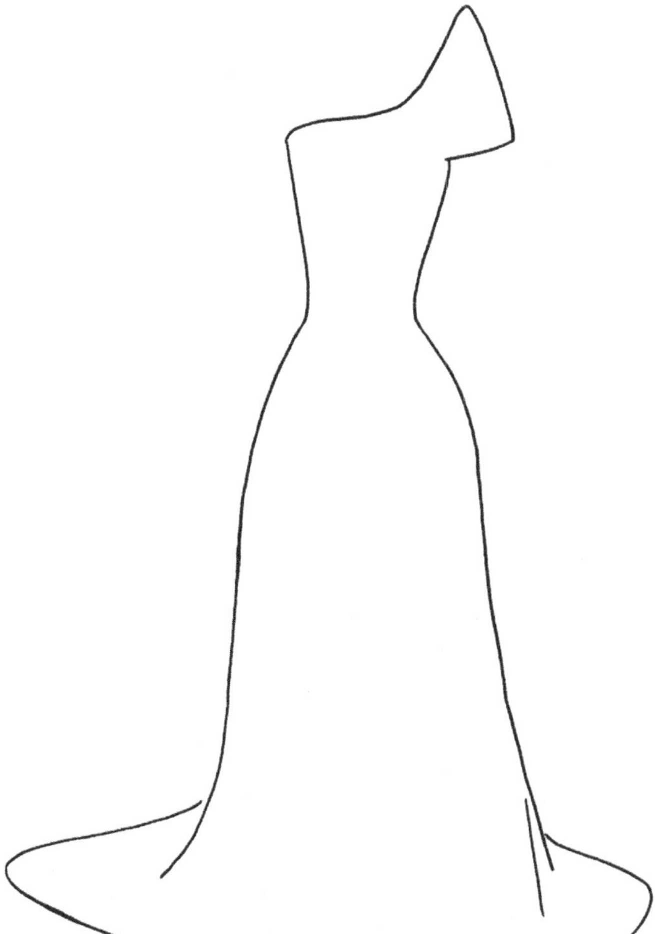

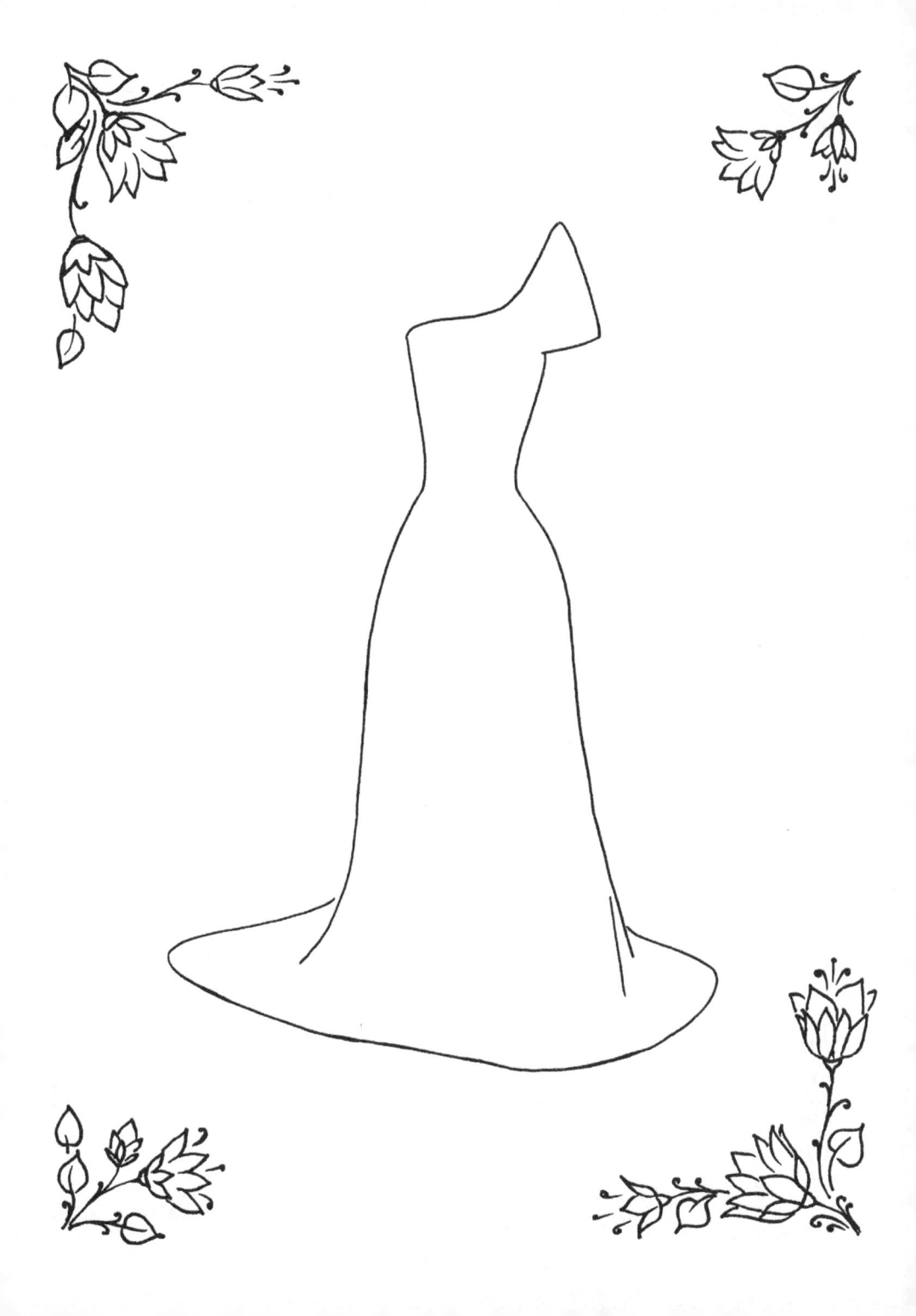

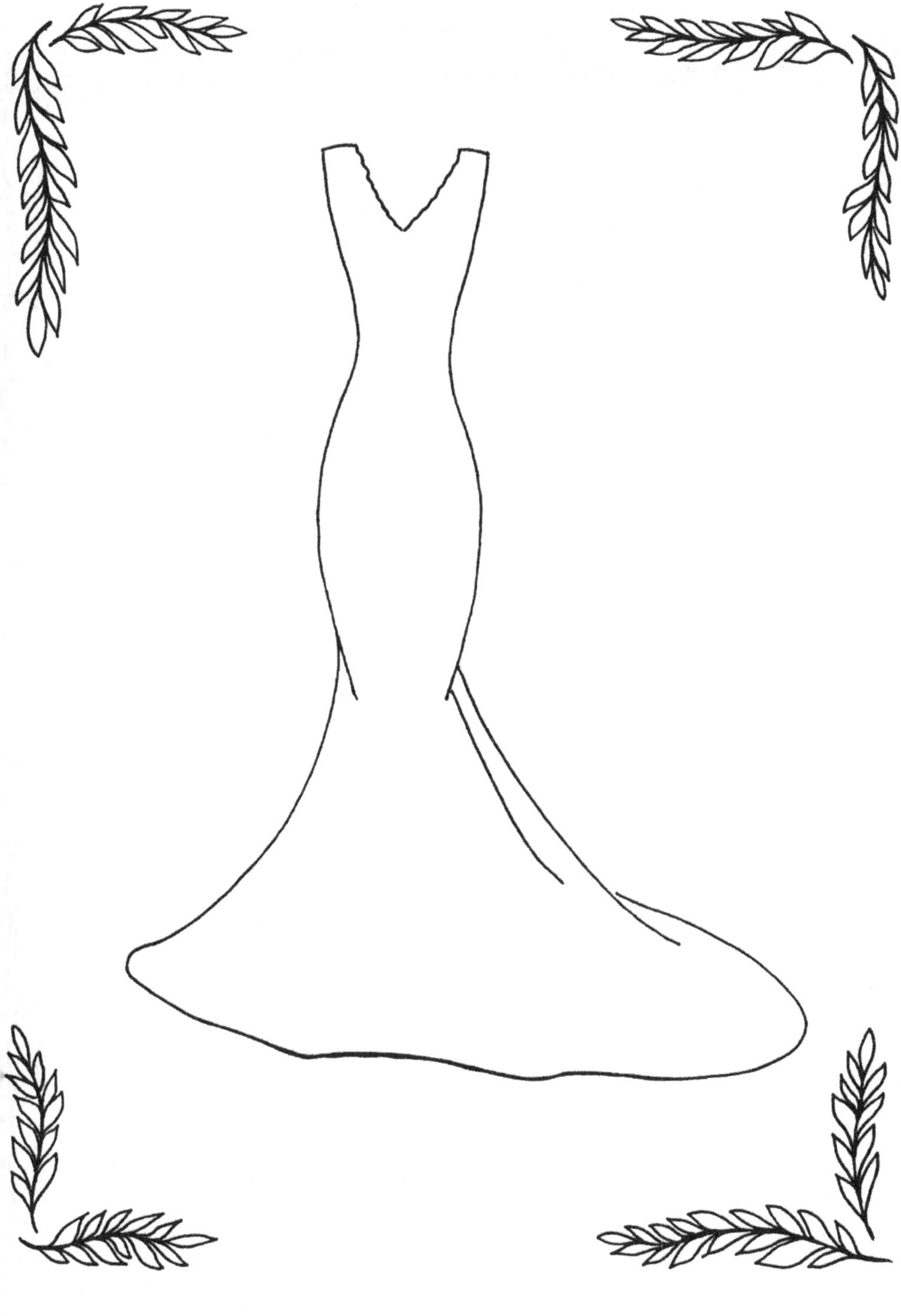

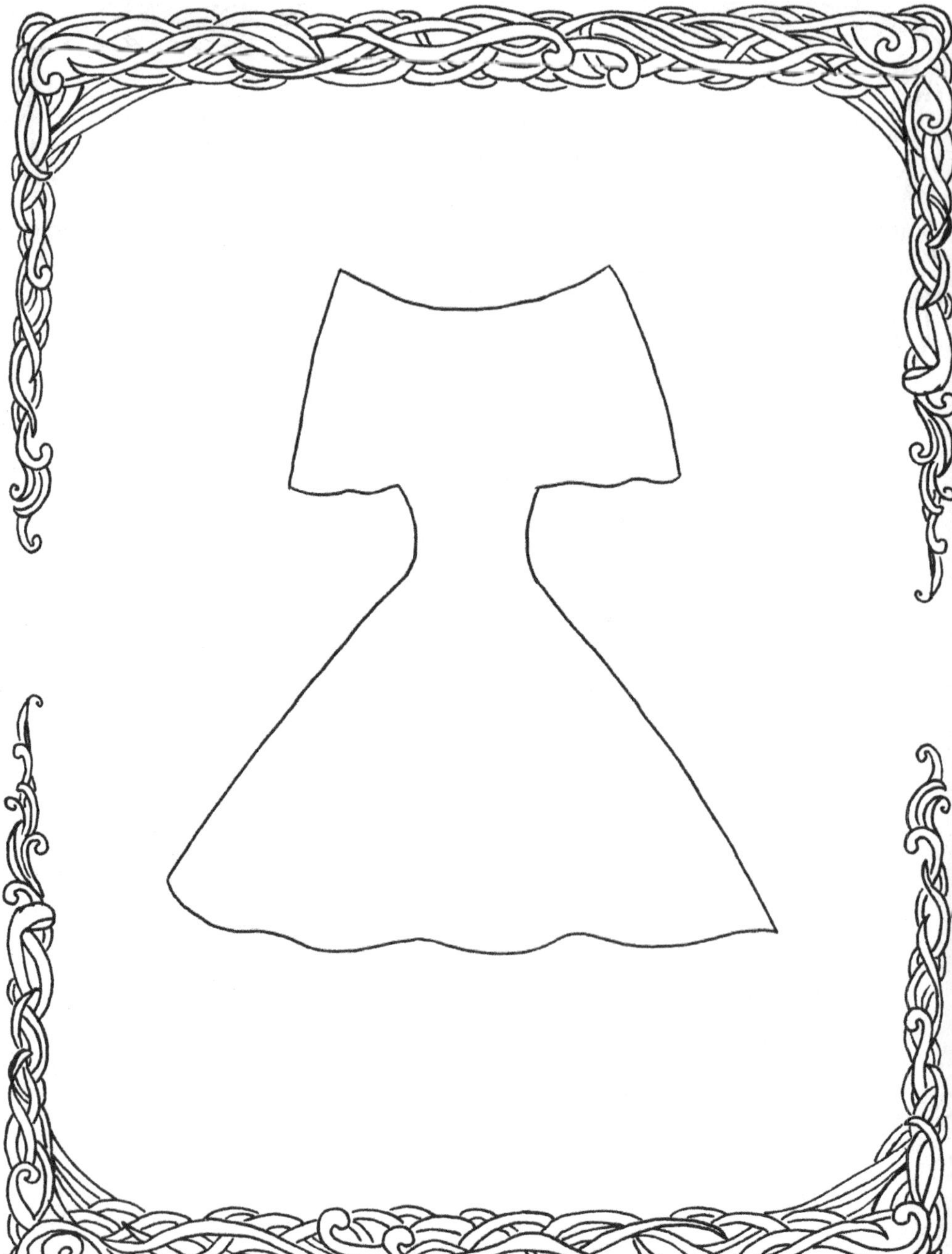

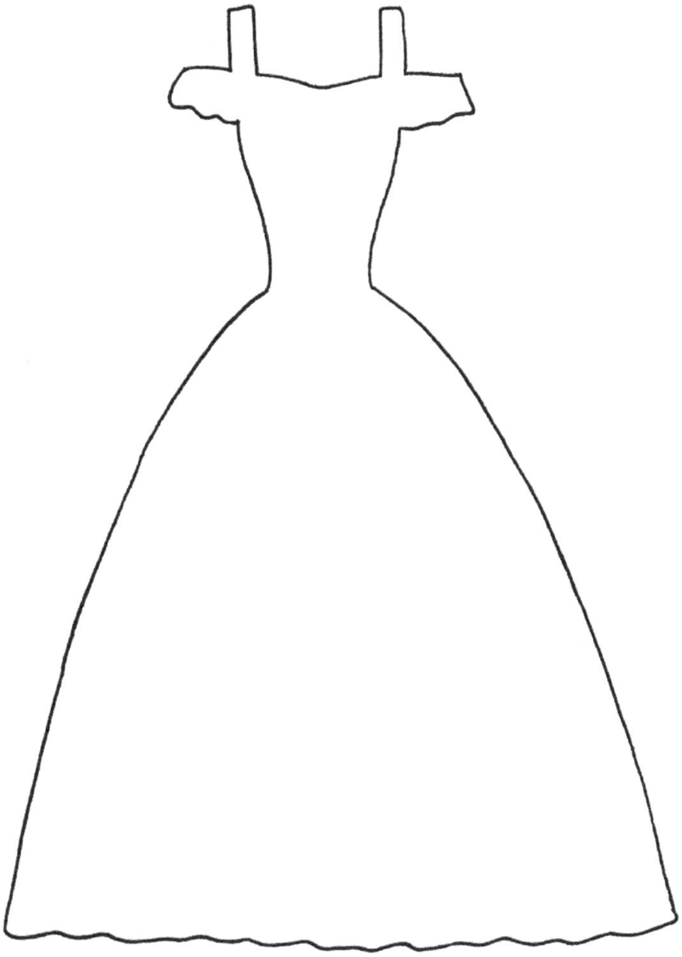

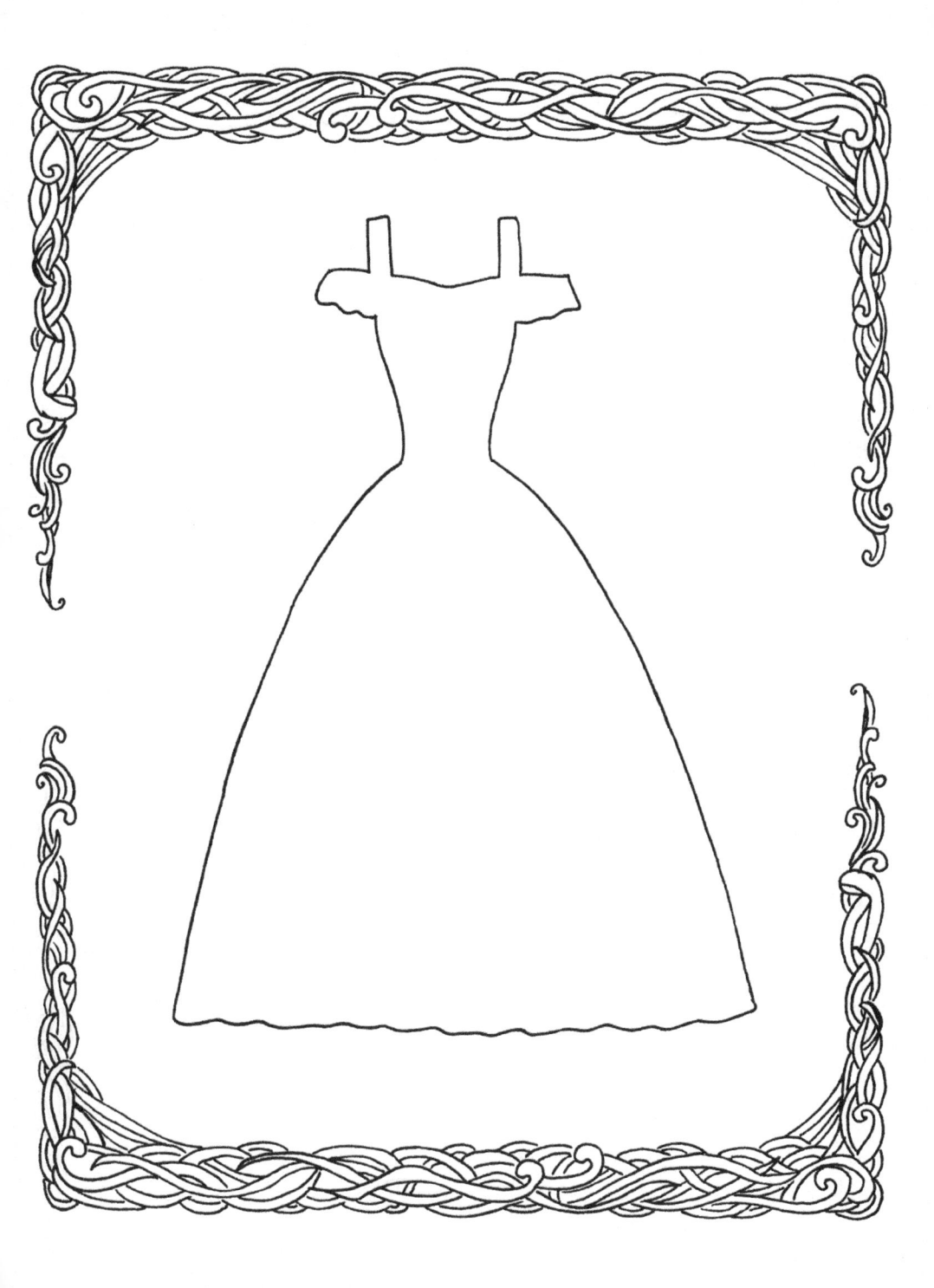

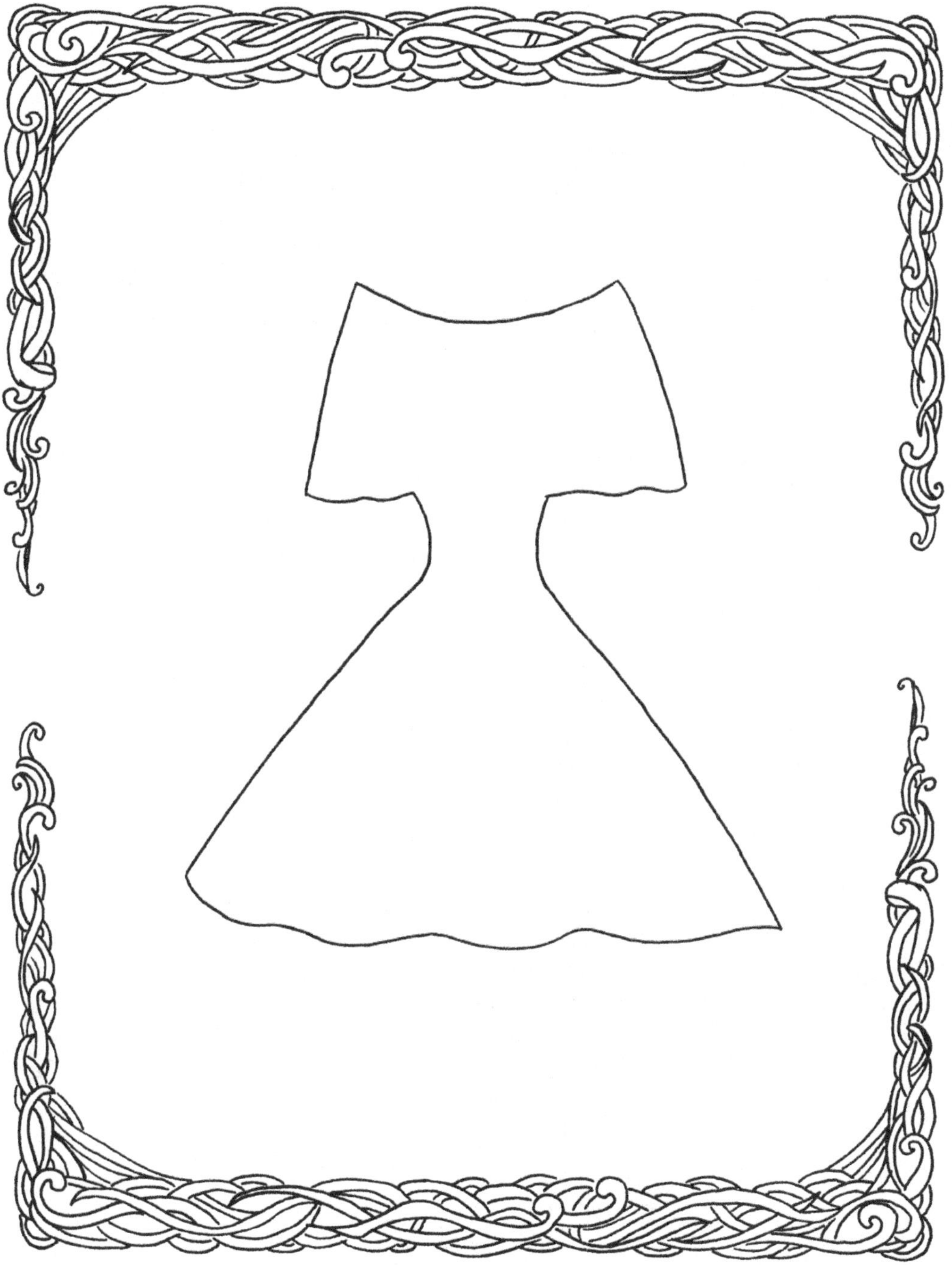

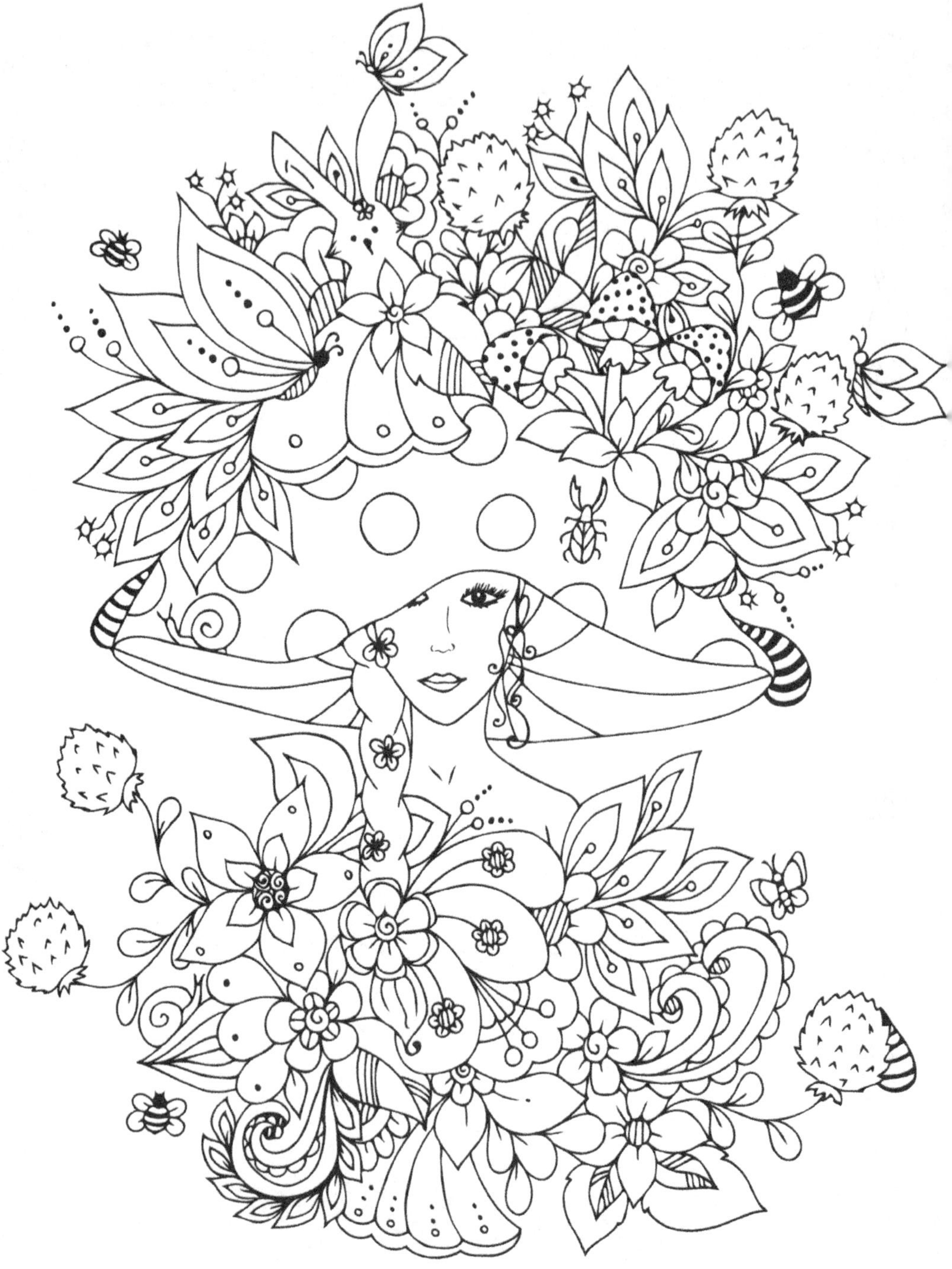

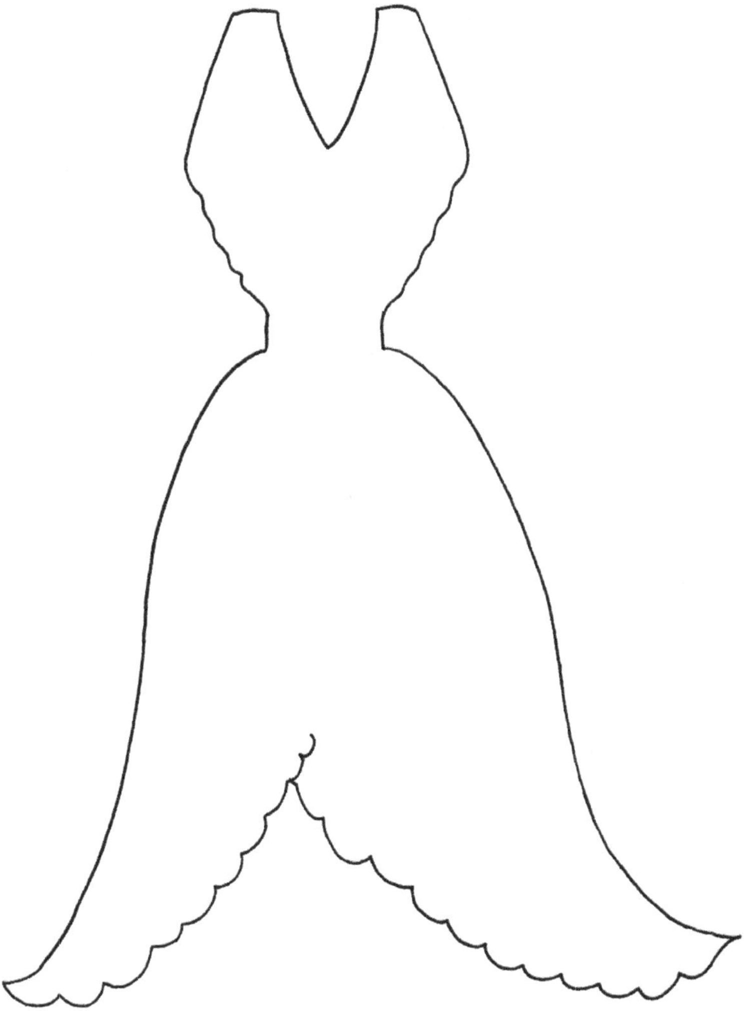

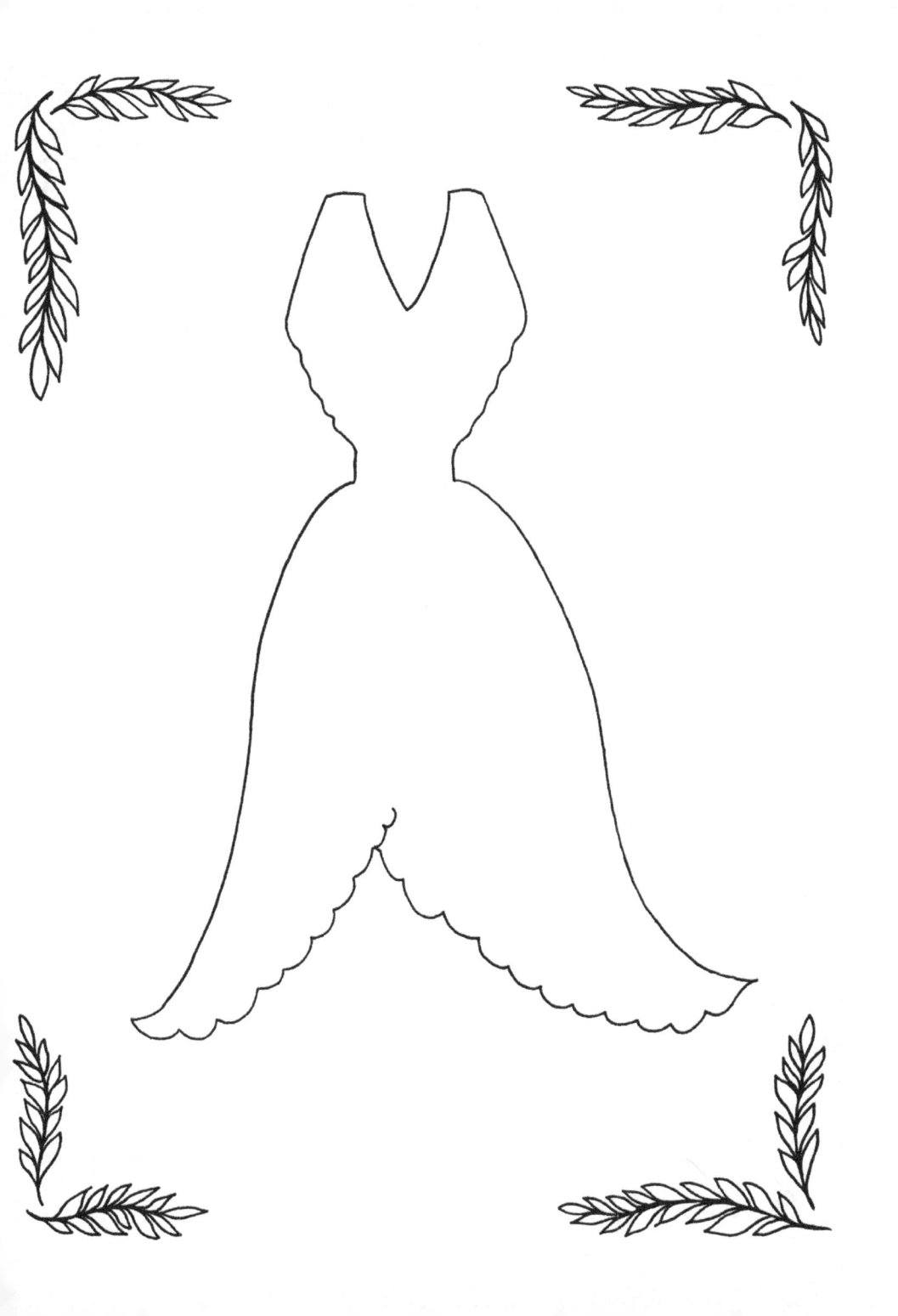

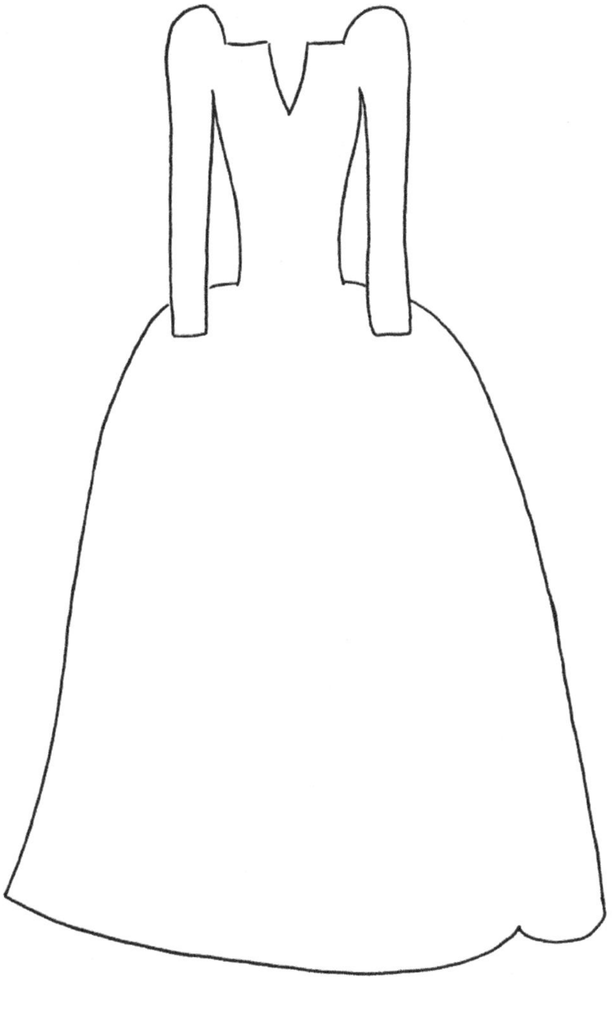

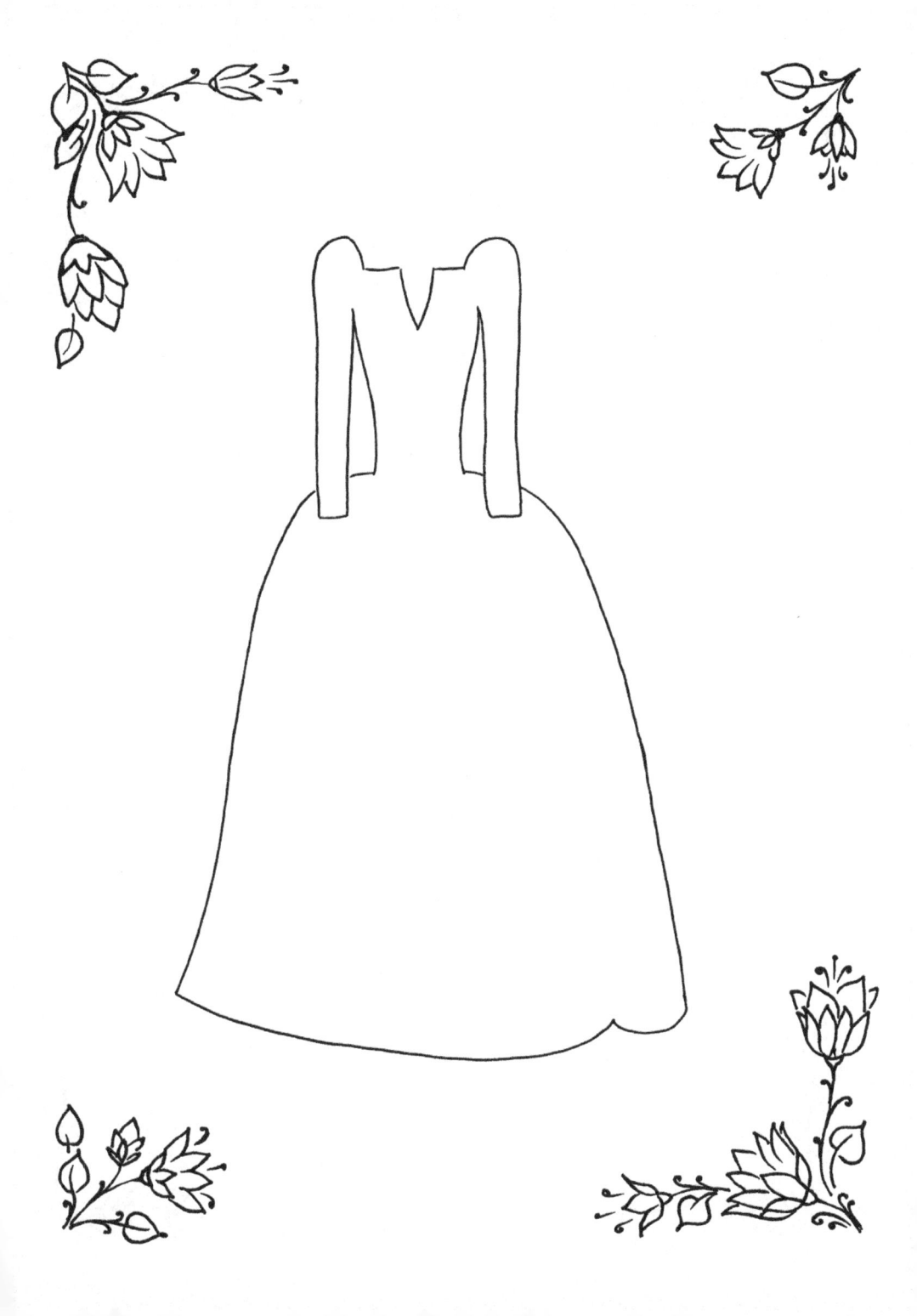

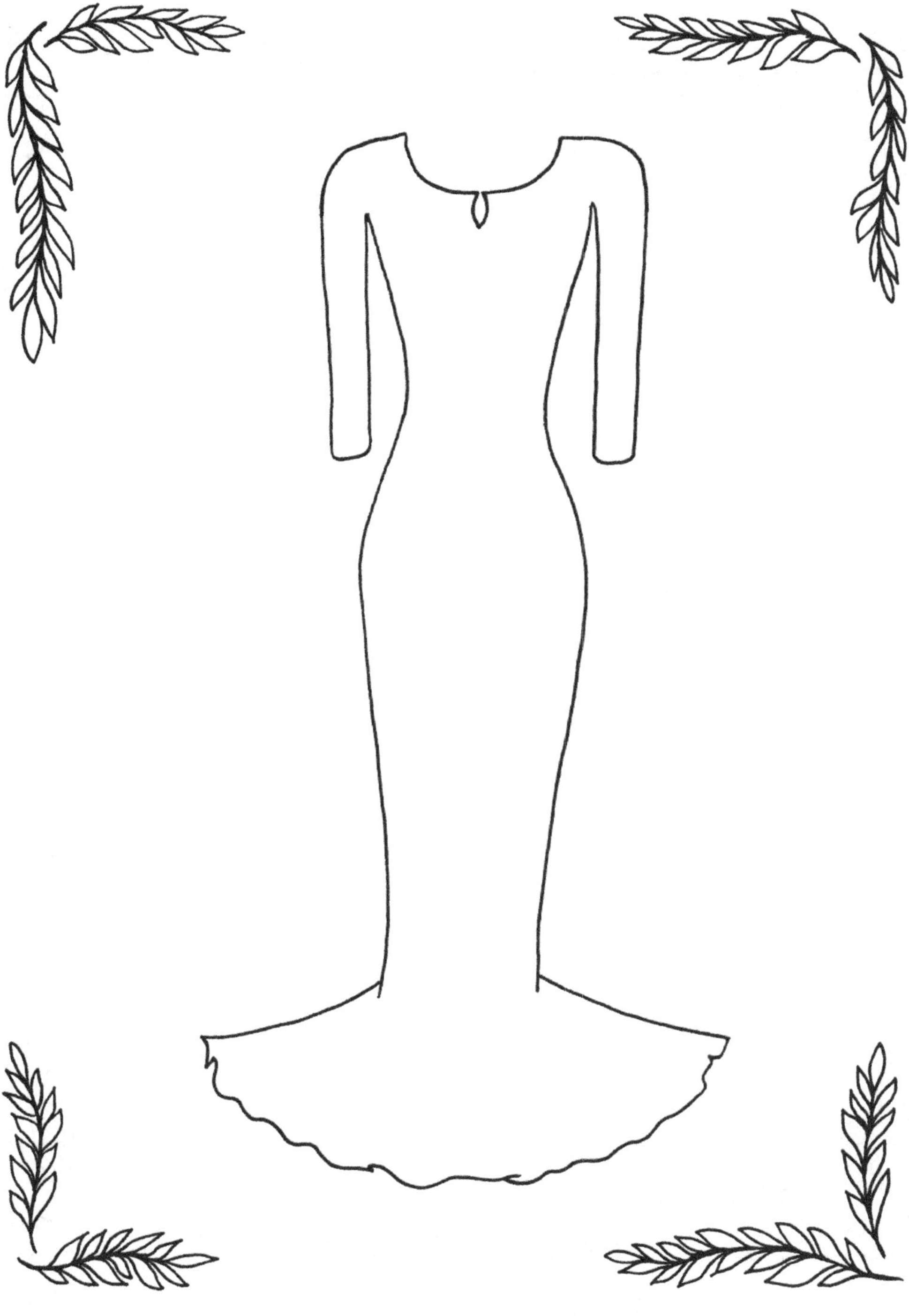

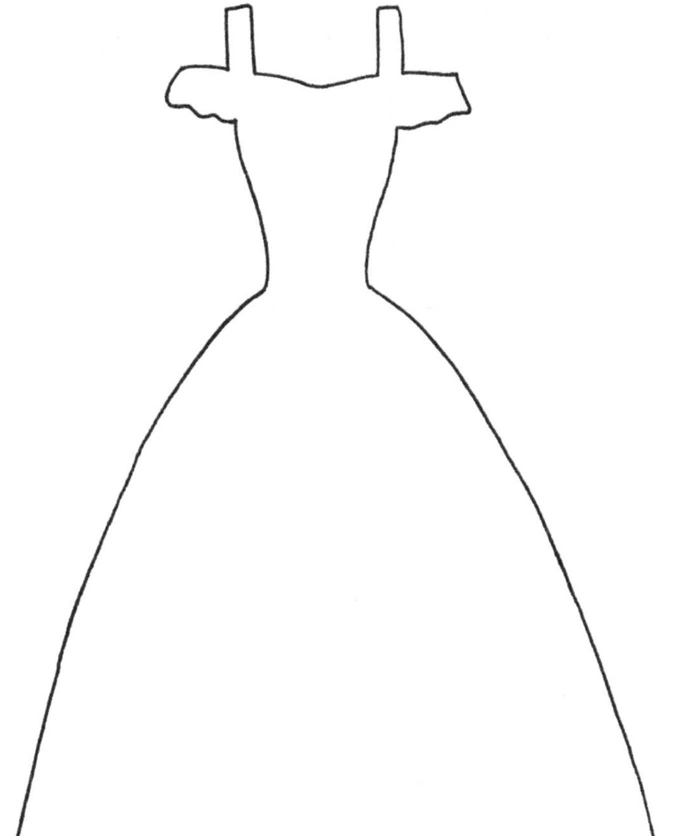

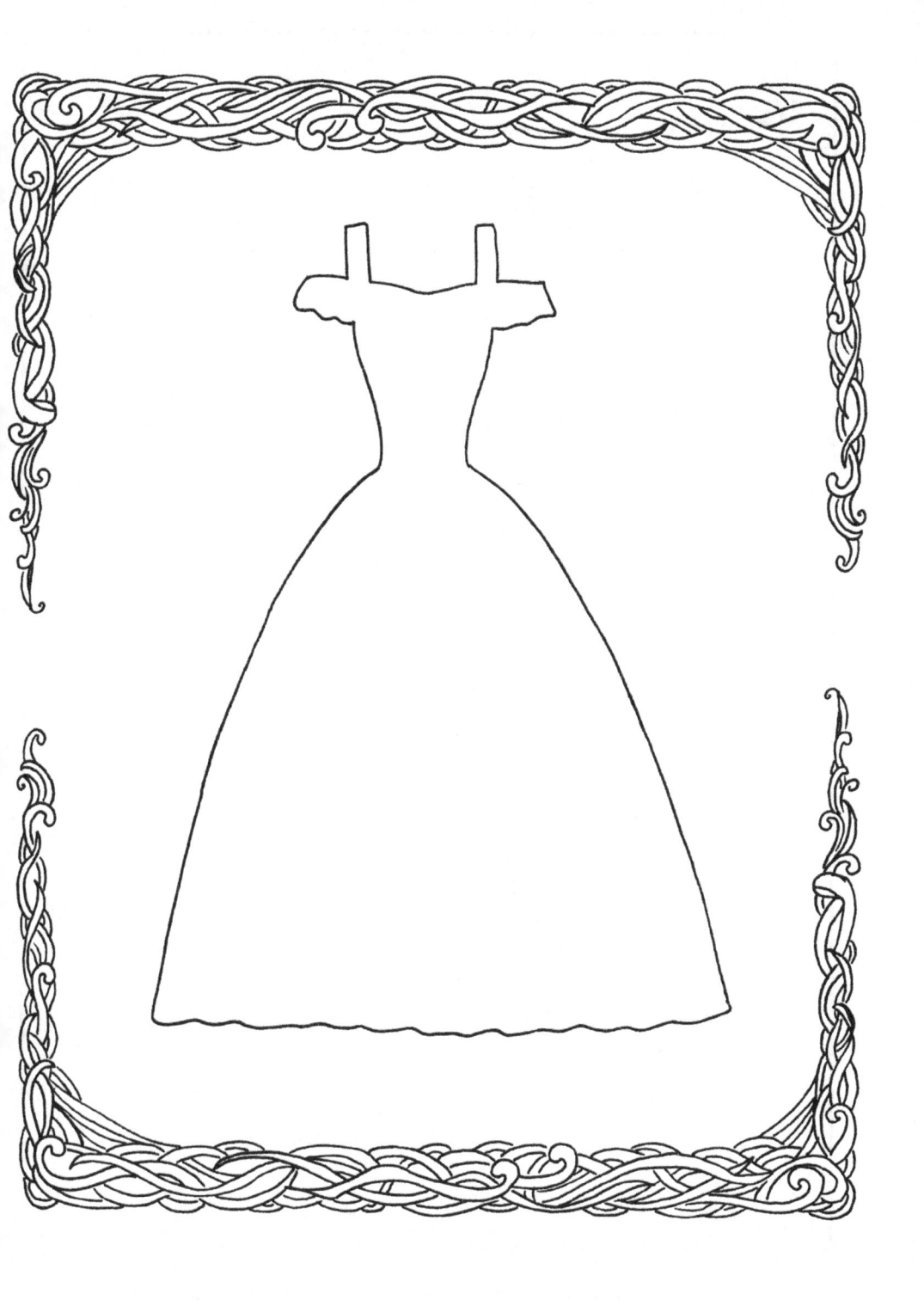

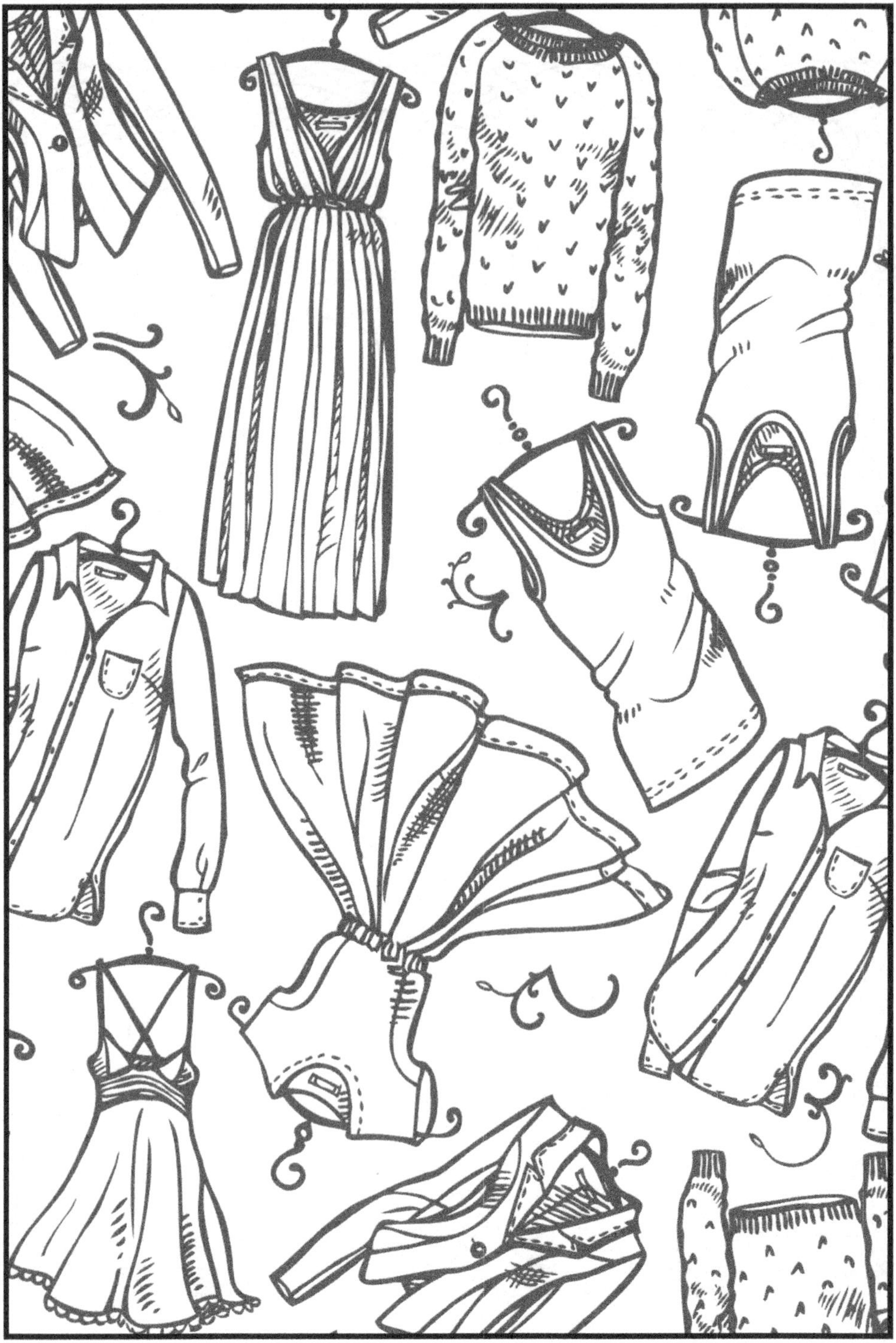

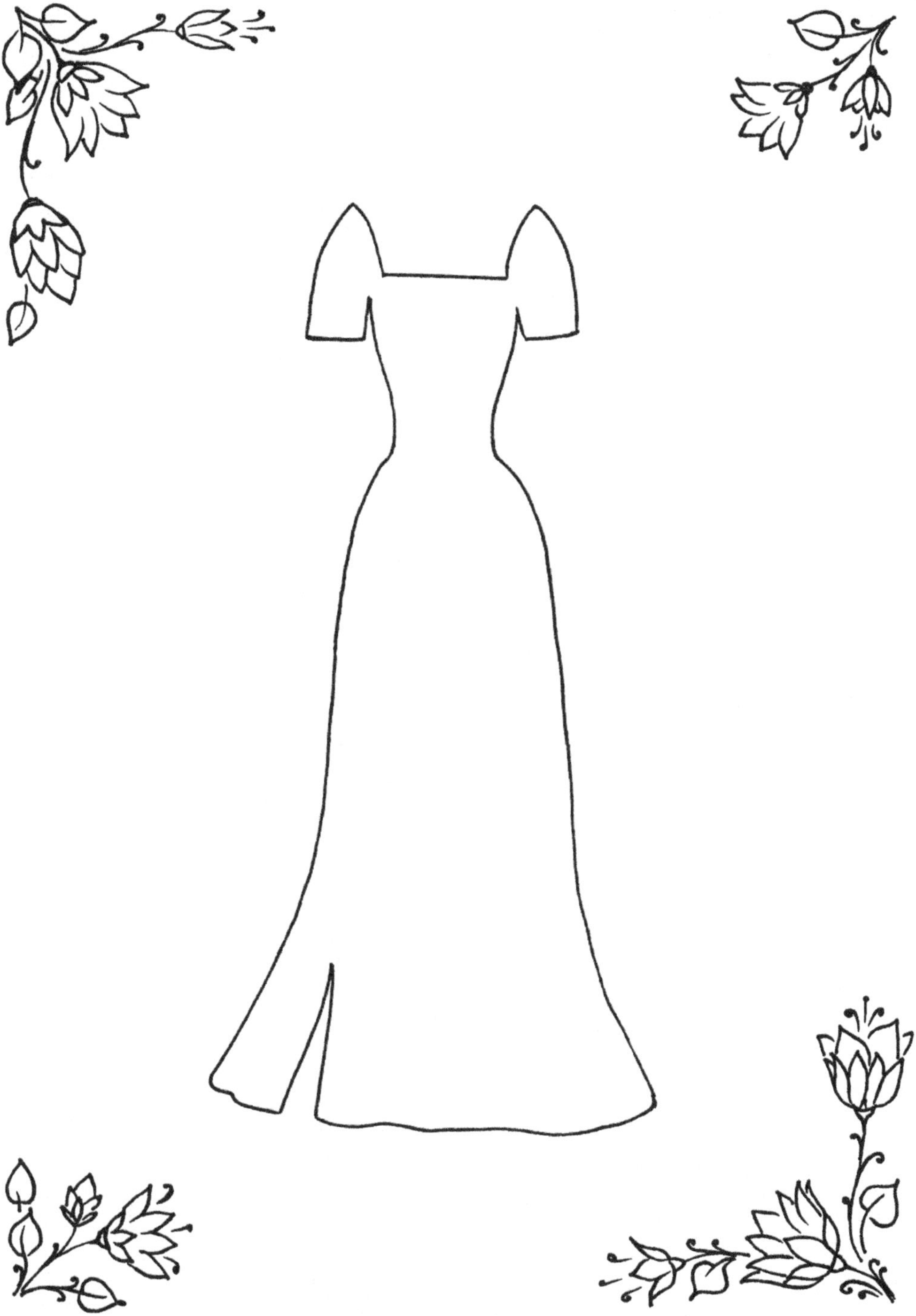

Made in the USA
Las Vegas, NV
22 December 2023